EXERCISES IN
ADVANCED AND SCHOLARSHIP LEVEL PRACTICAL
CHEMISTRY

EXERCISES IN
ADVANCED AND SCHOLARSHIP LEVEL PRACTICAL CHEMISTRY

SYSTÈME INTERNATIONAL UNITS
AND SYSTEMATIC NOMENCLATURE THROUGHOUT

DAVID ABBOTT M.A., Ph.D., Dip. Ed.

*SOMETIME SCHOLAR OF DOWNING COLLEGE, CAMBRIDGE
DEPUTY HEAD, THE GARTH HILL SCHOOL, BRACKNELL,
BERKSHIRE*

HULTON EDUCATIONAL PUBLICATIONS

1973 © D. Abbott
ISBN 0 7175 0643 6

*First Published 1973 by Hulton Educational Publications Ltd.,
Raans Road, Amersham, Bucks.*

Printed in Great Britain by
Billing & Sons Limited, Guildford and London

FOREWORD

by

Dr Arthur Finch, *Chief Examiner, London University Schools Examination Board.*

The operation of practical classes for Advanced Level chemistry courses poses formidable problems for teachers. In the first place, the syllabus is, in practice, so open that it is usually impossible to be certain that all material has been covered; representative exercises are sorely needed. Second, since it is usually agreed that unification of theory and practice is desirable, then experiments cannot be restricted to isolated skills such as volumetric expertise or to the aqueous chemistry of a relatively limited number of common anions and cations. Finally, teacher assessment of practical ability is being seriously studied and experiments capable of functioning as such exercises are desirable.

This book should prove very helpful both in its range and in depth. Like all good practical tests, it reflects the practical experience of its author, whose personal experience over many years is evident. It is a pleasure to recommend it to pupils and teachers and to express the hope that the art and science of quantitative chemistry which it so clearly encourages, will continue to attract the efforts of able scholars.

ARTHUR FINCH

ACKNOWLEDGMENTS

Full acknowledgment is made to all those examination boards mentioned in the first part of this book.

Full acknowledgment and thanks are made to Dr. R.D. Gidden, Head of Chemistry, The Leys School, for his work and expertise on several of the experiments, most notably B5, B8, C1, C7, D9 and exercise 28 (Organic). Acknowledgment is also made to Dr. A. Finch for his encouragement throughout preparation.

PREFACE

Over the past decade the format of advanced level practical chemistry examinations has changed radically, and for the better. At one time, all that the teacher had to ensure was that his or her students for this examination practised routine titrations week after week and then managed to learn up sufficient of their qualitative analysis tables to carry them through the second question.

It is still true to say that titrations form a very important part of the advanced level practical course, but the experiments set nowadays are much more interesting, both from the point of view of experimental procedure and from the point of view of calculation. Books are often allowed in the examinations and so less material has to be retained in the minds of the students and actual competence at experimental work can be tested. Also, simple observation/ inference/preparation experiments involving organic materials have crept into the examination papers and this has brightened the teaching of organic chemistry in general. Two by two radical mixtures of inorganic salts are seldom (if ever) set in modern examinations, being replaced by a simple salt analysis or an investigation type of experiment, which seems to be a much better test of a candidate's ability to think.

Now what does all this mean to the teacher of chemistry as far as preparation for his practical classes is concerned? He or she has to prepare his/her candidates to deal with some types of experiment in physical chemistry (e.g. reaction kinetics, stoichiometry, distribution law, thermochemistry, solubility), as well as dealing with a less routine type of titration, a sequence of simple salt analyses and observation/inference exercises for both organic and inorganic materials.

The idea of this little book is to provide the student with clear directions for performing such experiments. It is felt that the book will be most useful during the examination year and in the final term before that year. As well as performing experiments of the type given in this book, students should also do a sequence of standard titration exercises, some organic preparations, some inorganic preparations and some more difficult physical chemistry experiments of the type which could not really be set in an examination (e.g. potentiometric titration, conductivity, gas chromatgraphy). It is hoped that the experiments included here will help both the teacher and the student. An attempt has been made to cover as wide a range of 'examinable' experiments as possible and also to enable the student to cover as wide a range of techniques as possible, for example, titration, syringe manipulation, distribution law, thermochemistry, reaction kinetics, solubility determinations, redox, simple salt analysis, observation/deduction on organic and inorganic compounds, recrystallisation, melting-point determination, simple preparations of organic compounds (acetylation, tosylation, diazotization, 3,5-dinitrobenzoylation etc.), chromatography, freezing-point determination, phase equilibria, gravimetric analysis, and inorganic preparations.

The best way for this book to be used is probably to make it understood that students do *not* consult the directions to supervisors (issued separately) until *after* they have attempted the experiment in question. It is expected that observation/deduction/preparation experiments will take approximately a single period, while a double period may be necessary for the analytical/physical chemistry experiments. Students should be encouraged to write up their results as they proceed and not leave this to be done at a later date, i.e. this is a book designed to train them in examination technique as well as giving them a wide range of experiments for their practical course. The value of such experiments to 'back up' classes on theoretical chemistry should not be underestimated.

DAVID ABBOTT

ACKNOWLEDGEMENTS

The author would like to offer his thanks to the following examination boards who have given permission to use questions taken from their recent examinations:

Oxford and Cambridge Joint Schools Examination Board (O. and C.)

Cambridge Open Scholarship and Entrance Examination (Cambridge Open Schol.)

London Schools Examination Board (L.)

Associated Examining Board (A.E.B.)

Northern Ireland Schools Examinations Board (N.I.)

Thanks are also due to Dr R. D. Gidden, Dr A. Finch (both for helpful advice) and Mr Leslie Wallis, Chief Technical Assistant at The Leys School, Cambridge, without whose constant advice and help on the practical side the experiments in this book would never have been tried so successfully.

Thanks must also be given to many Sixth Formers at The Leys School whose successes and failures in these experiments have enabled, it is hoped, a reasonable standard to be set.

GRADING OF EXPERIMENTS ACCORDING TO DIFFICULTY

Experiments are graded by means of asterisks according to the difficulty experienced in doing them by students of average ability.

* Easily done by most students.

** Reasonably easy to perform but the calculation or interpretation may well prove difficult to some students.

*** Quite difficult to perform and also having a tricky calculation/interpretation.

CONTENTS

Mr Leslie Wallis, Chief Technician, The Leys School, Cambridge, demonstrates an organic preparation. Mr Wallis has demonstrated experiments at The Leys School since 1933.

Photo: Terry Penny

ANALYTICAL AND
PHYSICAL CHEMISTRY EXERCISES

The general topics covered within this section are as follows:

A   Atomic Weights (Relative Atomic Masses), Molar Reacting Weights and Stoichiometry
B   Solubility, Solubility Product, Partition Law and Ionic Theory
C   Chemical Kinetics
D   Thermal Chemistry

Unless otherwise instructed, set out titration results like this:

	Volume solution I (in pipette): cm^3	Burette readings initial	final	Difference in burette readings, i.e. volume of solution II added: cm^3
Rough	25·00	0·0	27·6	27·6
Accurate	25·00	0·10	27·45	27·35
	25·00	2·25	29·65	27·40

Average of accurate titration figures
(quoted to 2 dec. places)
$\frac{1}{2}(27\cdot35+27\cdot40) = 27\cdot38$ cm^3

Note: IM solution $= 1$ mol dm^{-3} solution

A1   Molar Reacting Weights (*)

Prepare a solution of copper (II) sulphate, $CuSO_4.5H_2O$, containing between 5·80 and 6·00 grammes in 250 cm^3 and use it to find the molarity of the solution of sodium thiosulphate, HA.

   HB is a solution containing 3·50 grammes per cubic decimetre of an oxidising substance. Find the formula weight of this substance. To 25 cm^3 portions of HB, and approximately 10 cm^3 of bench dilute sulphuric acid, followed by 10 cm^3 (an excess) of potassium

1

iodide solution (ten per cent). Then titrate this solution against HA from the burette. You are told that one mole of the oxidising substance liberates three moles of iodine from an excess of potassium iodide in acidic solution.

A2 Molar Reacting Weights (**)

The given compound A1 is an acid oxalate (ethanedioate) $KH_x(C_2O_4)_y.zH_2O$ of formula weight 254·2.

- (a) Prepare a standard solution containing 1·5–1·6 g of A1 in 250 cm^3.
- (b) Titrate the A1 solution with the standard sodium hydroxide solution A2 whose concentration you will be told.
- (c) Titrate the A1 solution with the solution A3 (standard potassium permanganate (manganate VII) whose concentration you will be told.

From your results, determine the values of x, y and z.

No detailed account of your experimental procedure is required but all relevant readings should be recorded and your calculations shown clearly.

(N.I.)

A3 Atomic Weights (Relative Atomic Masses (**)

(a) Prepare a standard solution of the iodate MIO_3 (A1) containing 1·10 to 1·20 g of the solid in 250 cm^3.

(b) Use the solution A1 to standardise the hydrochloric acid A2. To 25 cm^3 of A2 add 1 g of potassium iodide and 25 cm^3 of A2. Titrate with the solution A3 whose concentration you will be told.

(c) To about 30 cm^3 of solution A1 add 1 g of potassium iodide and about 3 g of sodium thiosulphate crystals. Add methyl red indicator and titrate with A2. The purpose of the sodium thiosulphate here is to remove the liberated iodine so that the colour of the methyl red can be seen.

$$IO_3^- + 5I^- + 6H^+ \rightarrow 3I_2 + 3H_2O$$

From your results, calculate the formula weight of the iodate MIO_3 and hence the atomic weight of the metal M.

(N.I.)

A4 Atomic Weights (Relative Atomic Masses) (*)

Weigh accurately between 1·5 and 2·0 g of the solid A1 into a 250 cm^3 beaker. A1 is a carbonate MCO_3.

Add to the beaker 50·0 (or 40·0) cm^3 of the hydrochloric acid A2, whose concentration you will be told. Take precautions to avoid loss of acid spray. When effervescence has ceased, boil the solution gently for about 120 s. Then leave the beaker to cool for at least 900 s.

Transfer the solution to a 250 (or 200) cm^3 graduated flask and make up to the mark with water.

Titrate portions of this solution with the standard sodium carbonate solution A3 whose concentration you will be told. Use screened methyl orange as indicator.

Calculate the atomic weight (relative atomic mass) of M.

Important—Record all weighings and burettè readings, and state the volume of your pipette and graduated flask.

(N.I.)

A5 Molar Reacting Weights (**)

You are provided with the following solutions:

HA is potassium permanganate (manganate(VII)), 0·02M
HB is ammonium iron(II) sulphate
HC is an aqueous solution of a substance C

(*a*) Take 20 cm^3 (or 25 cm^3) of solution HB and titrate with HA from a burette. From your results, calculate the molarity of HB.

$$MnO_4^- + 5Fe^{2+} + 8H^+ \rightarrow Mn^{2+} + 5Fe^{3+} + 4H_2O$$

(*b*) Take 20 cm^3 (or 25 cm^3) of HB in a conical flask, add 10 cm^3 of HC, and titrate the mixture with HA. From your results, calculate the apparent molarity of the mixture as a reducing agent. Calculate the reducing power as if it were ammonium iron(II) sulphate.

(*c*) Repeat procedure (*b*), using 20 cm^3 of HC, then 30 cm^3, and finally 40 cm^3.

Plot your results on a graph, with molarity of the mixture as a reducing agent as ordinate against the volume of HC added as abscissa.

(*d*) Comment on the form of the graph and say what you think substance C might be.

Observations of what takes place in the various reactions and titrations should be recorded and used to help you in part (*d*).

A6 Molar Reacting Weights (**)

HA   is an aqueous solution of ammonium iron(II) sulphate, the exact concentration of which is given by the teacher.

HB   is an aqueous solution of sodium hydroxide, the exact concentration of which is given by the teacher.

HC   is an aqueous solution of unknown concentration of potassium permanganate (manganate(VII)).

HD   is an aqueous solution of unknown concentration containing oxalic (ethanedioic) acid and sodium oxalate (ethanedioate).

(*a*) Standardise the potassium permanganate solution against the ammonium iron(II) sulphate solution as follows:

Take 25 cm^3 (or 20 cm^3) of the ammonium iron(II) sulphate solution HA in a conical flask, add an equal volume of dilute sulphuric acid and titrate with potassium permanganate solution HC until a permanent faint pink colour appears. Repeat the titration until two consistent readings are obtained. Express your result in moles per cubic decimetre. The overall equation for the reaction is

$$MnO_4^- + 5Fe^{2+} + 8H^+ \rightarrow Mn^{2+} + 5Fe^{3+} + 4H_2O$$

(b) Determine the concentrations of oxalic (ethanedioic) acid and of sodium oxalate (ethanedioate) in solution HD as follows:

(i) Take 25 cm³ (or 20 cm³) of solution HD in a conical flask and titrate with sodium hydroxide solution HB using phenolphthalein as indicator. Repeat until two consistent readings are obtained. Calculate the concentration of oxalic acid in solution HD in moles per cubic decimetre *and* in grammes per cubic decimetre.

(ii) Take 25 cm³ (or 20 cm³) of solution HD in a conical flask, add an equal volume of dilute sulphuric acid and heat to 333 to 343 K. Titrate the hot solution on with potassium permanganate solution (maintaining the temperature between 333 and 343 K by reheating if necessary) until a faint pink colour persists for 30 seconds. Repeat until two consistent readings are obtained. Calculate the total oxalate concentration in solution HD in moles per cubic decimetre and thence the concentration of sodium oxalate in moles per cubic decimetre *and* in grammes per cubic decimetre.

The overall equation for the reactions is

$$2MnO_4^- + 5C_2O_4^{2-} + 16H^+ \rightarrow 2Mn^{2+} + 10CO_2 + 8H_2O$$

Set out your results like this:

Concentrations given by teacher:

HA (ammonium iron(II) sulphate)...........

HB (sodium hydroxide)...........

Volume of pipette used: ....

(a) *Standardisation of potassium permanganate solution against ammonium iron(II) sulphate solution*

Titration values: Mean titre...........

Concentration of potassium permanganate
solution HC in moles/cubic decimetre: ....

(b) *Determination of the concentrations of oxalic (ethanedioic) acid and of sodium oxalate (ethanedioate) in solution HD*

(i) Titration values: Mean titre...........
(sodium hydroxide)

Concentration of oxalic acid in
solution HD in moles/cubic decimetre: ....

Concentration of oxalic acid in
   solution HD in g/cubic decimetre: . . . .

(ii) Titration values: Mean titre. . . . .
   (potassium permanganate)
Total oxalate concentration in
   solution HD in moles/cubic decimetre: . . . .
Sodium oxalate concentration in
   solution HD in moles/cubic decimetre: . . . .
Sodium oxalate concentration in
   solution HD in g/cubic decimetre: . . . .

                                       (O. and C.)

A7 Molar Reacting Weights (***)

You are required to determine the concentration (in grammes/cubic decimetre) of hydrazinium sulphate (N_2H_4, H_2SO_4) in solution X. The following procedure is recommended; it is based on the observation that hydrazine is oxidised quantitatively by bromate (V) ion in acidic solution, according to the equation

$$3N_2H_4 + 2BrO_3^- \rightarrow 3N_2 + 6H_2O + 2Br^-$$

(a) Transfer 25 cm^3 of solution X to a 500 cm^3 conical flask. Add in succession 50 cm^3 of *standard* potassium bromate solution (solution Y) and *ca.* 40 cm^3 of 3M hydrochloric acid. Close the flask immediately with a small inverted beaker and mix its contents by swirling. Allow the reactants to stand undisturbed at room temperature for 900 s and then add *ca.* 10 cm^3 of 10% potassium iodide solution. Titrate the liberated iodine with sodium thiosulphate solution (solution Z).

(b) Transfer 25 cm^3 of solution Y to a 250 cm^3 conical flask. Add *ca.* 10 cm^3 of 10% potassium iodide solution and *ca.* 20 cm^3 of 3M hydrochloric acid. Titrate the liberated iodine with solution Z.

       ($KBrO_3 = 167$; N_2H_4, $H_2SO_4 = 130$)

                                (Cambridge Open Schol.)

A8 Molar Reacting Weights and Atomic Weights (*)

Make a solution of the pure potassium chloride provided, containing approximately 1·90 to 2·10 grammes in 250 cm³. Use this solution to determine the molarity of the silver(I) nitrate provided, HA.

Solution HB contains 6·00 grammes per cubic decimetre of a salt of formula XCl_2. Use solution HA to determine

(i) the molar weight (relative molecular mass) of the compound XCl_2,

(ii) the atomic weight (relative atomic mass) of X.

A9 Molar Reacting Weights (*)

Make up a solution of borax ($Na_2B_4O_7.10H_2O$) from the pure solid provided, having between 4·40 and 4·60 grammes per 250 cm³. Titrate 25 cm³ portions of this solution with solution HA, which is hydrochloric acid, using screened methyl orange as indicator.

Use the now standard HA to determine the molarity of solution HB, which contains sodium hydroxide. Calculate the grammes per cubic decimetre of HB.

(*Note:* have HA in the burette in both titrations.)

A10 Reacting Volumes (*)

You are supplied with solutions of $KMnO_4$ (labelled X), acidified $FeSO_4$ (Y) and acidified H_2O_2 (Z). Put solution X in the burette.

(*a*) Using the measuring vessel supplied, transfer 10 cm³ of Y to a small flask and titrate it with X. The first sign of permanent pink in the mixture signifies the end-point. Repeat this titration—and all subsequent titrations—*only* if you are dissatisfied with it. *Extreme* accuracy will not be expected in this exercise.

(*b*) In a similar manner to the above operation, titrate 10 cm³ of Z with X.

(c) Make up the following mixtures of Y and Z.

cm^3 of Y	$+cm^3$ of Z
8·0	2·0
6·0	4·0
4·5	5·5
3·5	6·5
2·0	8·0

You will find it easiest to measure out the volume of Y from a burette into a marked vessel and then add Z up to the 10 cm^3 mark.

Titrate each of these mixtures with X. Set out all titrations in tabular form.

Draw a graph showing how the volume of X used varies with the volume of Y taken.

Deduce, from the graph, the volume of Y that just reacts with a stated volume of Z—i.e. their reacting volumes.

(O. and C.)

A11   Stoichiometry (**)

Iodine reacts with 1,3-dihydroxybenzene, $C_6H_4(OH)_2$, to give a substituted iodo-derivative. Determine the number of iodine atoms in the derivative formed when the iodination is carried out in aqueous potassium iodide solution at pH 5.

HA   is a solution of sodium thiosulphate.
HB   is a solution of iodine and potassium iodide.
HC   is a solution of 1,3-dihydroxybenzene.
HD   is an acetic (ethanoic) acid/sodium acetate (ethanoate) buffer solution.

The exact molarities of solutions HA and HC will be given by the teacher.

(a) Determine the molar concentration of iodine in solution HB as follows. Using a burette, or a pipette with a safety attachment, measure out 25 cm^3 of solution HB into a conical flask and titrate against the sodium thiosulphate solution HA adding starch solution as indicator near the end-point. Repeat this procedure until two consistent titres are obtained. From your results calculate the molarity of the iodine solution HB.

(b) Examine the iodination of 1,3-dihydroxybenzene at pH 5 in aqueous potassium iodide as follows:

Put approximately 100 cm^3 of the buffer solution HD into a conical flask. Using a burette, or a pipette with a safety attachment, add 25 cm^3 of the solution HC and 50 cm^3 of the iodine solution HB. After about 300 s titrate the residual iodine with the sodium thio-sulphate solution HA. Starch solution should be added when the brown colour of the iodine begins to fade and the end-point should be taken as the disappearance of the intense colour of the starch/iodine complex; a pink colour will remain in the solution after the end-point. Repeat this procedure until two constant titres are obtained.

From your results calculate the number of moles of residual iodine and hence the number of moles of iodine which react with one mole of 1,3-dihydroxybenzene under these conditions. Give the equation for the reaction.

(c) What would you expect to be the structural formula of iodo-derivative?

Set out your results like this:

Molarity of solution HA............

Molarity of solution HC............

(a) *Standardisation of solution HB*

Final level
Initial level
Titre   Mean titre........ cm^3
                      Molarity of solution HB............

(b) *The iodination of 1,3-dihydroxybenzene at pH 5*

Final level
Initial level
Titre   Mean titre........ cm^3
         Molarity of iodine remaining after
            reaction   ....
         Number of moles of 1,3-dihydroxy-
            benzene used for each titration   ....

Number of moles of iodine consumed
by 1,3-dihydroxybenzene in each
titration ....

Mole ratio, iodine:
1,3-dihydroxybenzene ....

Equation:

(c) *The structural formula of the iodo-derivative is probably:*

(O. and C.)

A12 Molar Reacting Weights (**)

Solution X is a solution of a compound containing sodium, iodine and oxygen only; you are given the molar concentration of iodine (I).

(*a*) Add 10 cm^3 of dilute sodium hydroxide and 20 cm^3 of 20-volume H_2O_2 to 25 cm^3 of X in a conical flask. Boil for about 1·2 ks, adding distilled water, if necessary, to prevent the solution boiling dry. Allow to cool. Add approximately 25 cm^3 of water, approximately 2 g of solid potassium iodide and about 10 cm^3 of dilute hydrochloric acid. Titrate the solution with standard sodium thiosulphate solution, L, using starch near the end-point.

(*b*) Make up a buffer solution of 10 g of borax in 250 cm^3 of water containing excess boric acid (about 15 g).

Add about 75 cm^3 of the buffer solution to 10 cm^3 of X in a conical flask. Add approximately 2 g of solid potassium iodide, leave for about 300 s and titrate the solution with the standard sodium thiosulphate L. Add a few cm^3 of concentrated hydrochloric acid to destroy the buffer and titrate again.

How do you interpret your observations?

(Cambridge Open Schol.)

A13 Molar Reacting Weights (**)

Prepare a solution of ammonium iron(II) sulphate, $(NH_4)_2SO_4$.

$FeSO_4.6H_2O$, containing between 8·80 and 9·00 grammes per 250 cm³. Using this solution, determine the molarity of the given solution, HX, of potassium permanganate (manganate(VII)).

Solution HY is a solution of an oxalate (ethanedioate) having a formula $XHC_2O_4.H_2C_2O_4.2H_2O$ and contains 7·00 g dm⁻³.

Titrate HY against HX and, from your results, determine the molar weight of the oxalate (enthanedioate) and also the relative atomic mass (atomic weight) of X. Show clearly each stage in your calculations.

A14   Molar Reacting Weights (***)

Determine the purity of a sample of potassium chlorate(V). 1·20 g of an impure sample of potassium chlorate was treated with 50·0 g of hydrated ammonium iron(II) sulphate, $(NH_4)_2SO_4.FeSO_4.6H_2O$, in acid solution until the reaction

$$KClO_3 + 6FeSO_4 + 3H_2SO_4 \rightarrow 3Fe_2(SO_4)_3 + KCl + 3H_2O$$

or

$$ClO_3^- + 6Fe^{2+} + 6H^+ \rightarrow 6Fe^{3+} + Cl^- + 3H_2O$$

was complete. This solution was then made up to 1 cubic decimetre. This, in all relevant respects, is the solution HA with which you are provided.

HB   is a solution of potassium permanganate (manganate(VII)).
HC   is a solution of sodium thiosulphate approximately 0·1M.

The exact molarity will be given by your teacher.

(a) Standardise the solution HB as follows:

To 25 cm³ (or 20 cm³) portions of solution HB in a conical flask add a roughly equal volume of dilute sulphuric acid and about 2 g (an excess) of solid potassium iodide. Titrate the liberated iodine with the solution HC, using starch indicator. Repeat until two consistent titres are obtained. From your results calculate the molarity of the potassium permanganate solution HB. The reaction between potassium permanganate and potassium iodide is:

$$2KMnO_4 + 10KI + 8H_2SO_4 \rightarrow 6K_2SO_4 + 2MnSO_4 + 8H_2O + 5I_2$$

or

$$2MnO_4^- + 10I^- + 16H^+ \rightarrow 2Mn^{2+} + 8H_2O + 5I_2$$

(b) Determine the concentration of unchanged ammonium iron(II) sulphate in solution HA by titration with the standardised solution of potassium permanganate (manganate(VII)). Use 25 cm^3 (or 20 cm^3) portions of HA in a conical flask, add a roughly equal volume of dilute sulphuric acid, and titrate with solution HB. Repeat until two consistent titres are obtained. The reaction between potassium permanganate (manganate(VII)) and ammonium iron(II) sulphate is essentially

$$2KMnO_4 + 10FeSO_4 + 8H_2SO_4 \rightarrow K_2SO_4 + 5Fe_2(SO_4)_3$$
$$+ 2MnSO_4 + 8H_2O$$

or

$$MnO_4^- + 8H^+ + 5Fe^{2+} \rightarrow 5Fe^{3+} + Mn^{2+} + 4H_2O$$

Calculate the molarity and concentration in g dm^{-3} of hydrated ammonium iron(II) sulphate in solution HA.

(c) Calculate the weight of potassium chlorate in g dm^{-3} in the original sample and hence the percentage purity.

Set out your results like this:

Volume of pipette used ....cm^3
Molarity of solution HC............

(a) *Standardisation of solution HB*

Final levels
Starting levels
Titres   Mean titre   .... cm^3
                                Molarity of HB............

(b) *Concentration of excess of ammonium iron(II) sulphate in solution*

Final levels
Starting levels
Titres   Mean titre........ cm^3
       Molarity of ammonium iron(II)
          sulphate hydrate in HA   ....
       Concentration of ammonium iron(II)
          sulphate hydrate in HA   ......g dm^{-3}

(c) *Purity of potassium chlorate sample*

Weight of potassium chlorate in original sample .... g

% purity............

(O. and C.)

A15   Molar Reacting Weights (**)

Solution A   contains 3.6 g of NaOH per cubic decimetre.

Solution B   contains 10.0 g of hydrated sodium carbonate per cubic decimetre, formula $Na_2CO_3.xH_2O$.

Solution C   contains approximately 1 mole of HCl per cubic decimetre.

A suitable indicator is provided.

(*a*) Standardise the hydrochloric acid solution C by titrating it against 25 cm³ portions of A.

Report the concentration of C as a molarity.

(*b*) Titrate 25 cm³ portions of B with the standardised hydrochloric acid and use your results to calculate the percentage by weight of *anhydrous* sodium carbonate present in the hydrated salt.

(*c*) From your results deduce the value of x in the formula $Na_2CO_3.xH_2O$.

(A.E.B.)

A16   Molar Reacting Weights (**)

A   is a hydrated barium salt of the formula $BaR_x.yH_2O$.

B   is a solution of A containing 12.5 g dm⁻³.

C   is a solution of sodium carbonate, approximately 0·1 M.

H   is hydrochloric acid, exactly 0·1 M.

(*a*) The salt A loses its water of crystallisation on heating. Determine the percentage loss in weight as follows. Take a weighed crucible, put into it about 2 grammes of A and weigh again. Heat the crucible *carefully* over a small hot bunsen flame for at least 3000 s and then allow to cool. Weigh the crucible and contents. Repeat the procedure until a constant weight is obtained.

During any waiting time, continue with the following experiments.

(*b*) Determine the exact molarity of C by titrating 20 cm³ (or 25 cm³) portions of it with the acid, H, using methyl orange or screened methyl orange as indicator.

(*c*) To 20 cm³ (or 25 cm³) of B add an equal volume of C. Heat the mixture gently until it is boiling. Allow to cool somewhat and filter off the precipitate of barium carbonate, *taking care to collect all the filtrate*. Wash the precipitate on the filter paper without removing it from the funnel with three separate quantities of water, adding the washings to the filtrate.

Titrate the filtrate and washings (not a portion of them) with the hydrochloric acid, H, using the same indicator as before.

(*d*) Calculate and tabulate the following:
  (i) the number of moles of sodium carbonate added to the portion of B in (*c*) above;
  (ii) the number of moles of sodium carbonate in the filtrate and washings;
  (iii) the number of moles of sodium carbonate used to precipitate the barium carbonate;
  (iv) the number of moles per cubic decimetre of B.

(*e*) What is the molar weight of A?

(*f*) Calculate the weight of water in one mole of the salt A.

(O. and C.)

A17 Molar Reacting Weights (**)

Solution HP contains 120 grammes per cubic decimetre of the salt P, $NaNH_4HPO_4.xH_2O$.

HQ is an approximately molar solution of sodium hydroxide.

HR is an exactly molar solution of hydrochloric acid.

(*a*) Determine the molarity of the sodium hydroxide solution HQ. Have the acid in the burette and use phenolphthalein as indicator.

(*b*) Put 20 cm³ (or 25 cm³) of the solution HP in a conical flask and add the same volume of sodium hydroxide solution HQ. Boil the mixture *gently*, taking care to avoid loss by spray, until you can no longer detect ammonia in the steam above the liquid. (This should take about 600 s.) Allow the solution to cool thoroughly, and titrate it with the hydrochloric acid HR, again using phenolphthalein as indicator. Make at least two determinations in this way.

(*c*) Calculate

(i) the weight of ammonia driven off by the action of the sodium hydroxide solution, using the equation:

$$NaNH_4HPO_4 + NaOH \rightarrow Na_2HPO_4 + NH_3 \uparrow + H_2O$$

or

$$NH_4HPO_4^- + OH^- \rightarrow HPO_4^{2-} + NH_3 \uparrow + H_2O$$

(ii) the concentration in grammes per cubic decimetre of the anhydrous salt in HP;

(iii) the weight of water of crystallisation in 120 grammes of the hydrated salt;

(iv) the value of x.

(O. and C.)

A18   Molar Reacting Weights (**)

HX is a solution of silver(I) nitrate, 0·1M.
HY is a solution of potassium bromide.
HZ is a solution of mercury(I) nitrate, $Hg_2(NO_3)_2.2H_2O$.
HV is a solution of eosin.

(*a*) Determine the molarity of the potassium bromide solution HY as follows:

Take 25 cm³ (or 20 cm³) of potassium bromide solution HY in a conical flask and add 10 drops of eosin solution HV as indicator. Run in silver nitrate solution HX from a burette, shaking the flask vigorously after each addition. A milky precipitate of silver(I) bromide is formed and this soon becomes faintly pink in colour. The end-point is quite sudden and occurs when the addition of a further drop of silver(I) nitrate causes the precipitate to flocculate and fall to the bottom assuming a magenta or lilac tint, with the supernatant liquid colourless or faintly cloudy.

Make one rough and two accurate determinations.

(Wash the precipitate out of the conical flask immediately after the titration to prevent staining of glassware.)

(b) Determine the concentration of mercury(I) nitrate solution HZ by the following method.

Measure out, by means of a burette, 24 cm³ of mercury(I) nitrate solution into a conical flask. Add 25 cm³ (or 25 cm³) of potassium bromide solution and shake the flask vigorously. Filter off the precipitate of mercury(I) bromide and wash the precipitate thoroughly with cold water. To the filtrate plus washings, add 10 drops of eosin and titrate the excess potassium bromide with silver(I) nitrate as described above. At the end-point the precipitate suddenly flocculates but in this case assumes a reddish tinge as it lies at the bottom of the flask. Make *two* determinations.

Calculate the molarity of the mercury(I) nitrate solution and from this the concentration in g dm^{-3} of the hydrated salt $Hg_2(NO_3)_2.2H_2O$.

$$AgNO_3 + KBr \rightarrow AgBr \downarrow + KNO_3$$

$$Hg_2(NO_3)_2 + 2KBr \rightarrow Hg_2Br_2 \downarrow + 2KNO_3$$

or

$$Ag^+ + Br^- \rightarrow AgBr \downarrow$$

$$Hg_2^{2+} + 2Br^- \rightarrow Hg_2Br_2 \downarrow$$

Note: The mercury(I) nitrate solution *must* be measured out with a burette.

(O. and C.)

A19 Molar Reacting Weights (**)

HF is a solution of oxalic (ethanedioic) acid exactly 0·05 M.
HG is a solution of potassium permanganate (manganate(VII)).
HH is a solution of hydrogen peroxide.

(a) Determine the molarity of the potassium permanganate (manganate(VII)) solution as follows:

To 25 cm^3 (or some standard volume) of ocalic (ethanedioic) acid solution HF in a conical flask add 10 cm^3 of dilute sulphuric acid and heat on a sand-bath until the flask is just too hot to hold comfortably on the hand. Run in potassium permanganate (manganate(VII)) until a faint pink colour persists.

(b) Take 25 cm^3 (or some standard volume) of the hydrogen peroxide solution HH in a conical flask; add 10 cm^3 of dilute sulphuric acid and titrate with potassium permanganate (manganate (VII)), *using no heat*, until a faint pink colour persists. Make *three* determinations.

The potassium permanganate (manganate(VII)) and hydrogen peroxide reduce each other.

$$2MnO_4^- + 5H_2O_2 + 10H^+ \rightarrow 2Mn^{2+} + 8H_2O + 5O_2 \uparrow$$

Determine the concentration of hydrogen peroxide in solution HH in g dm^{-3}.

(c) If solution HH was prepared from a more concentrated solution of hydrogen peroxide by diluting 5 cm^3 with 95 cm^3 of water, calculate the 'volume strength' of the original solution. This is the number of cm^3 of oxygen at s.t.p. that can be obtained from I cm^3 of the hydrogen peroxide solution.

(O. and C.)

A20   Molar Reacting Weights (**)

The solution X contains both iron(II) and iron(III). You are required to determine the ratio of the molar concentrations of these two ions. The following method is recommended.

(a) Titrate 25 cm^3 aliquots of X (note this solution has already been acidified with sufficient sulphuric acid for both titrations) with the standard potassium permanganate (manganate(VII)) solution Y. Keep the resultant solution for titration (b) below.

(b) To the solution from titration (a) above, add 15 cm^3 of the ammonium thiocyanate solution provided. Then titrate with the standard mercury(I) nitrate solution Z until the intense red colour, due to the formation of a complex between iron(III) and thiocyanate ions, fades and finally disappears. Thorough shaking is necessary near the end-point.

In the presence of thiocyanate ions, the following redox reaction occurs:

$$Hg_2^{2+} + 2Fe^{3+} \rightarrow 2Hg^{2+} + 2Fe^{2+}$$

Note: $KMnO_4 = 158$ $Hg_2(NO_3)_2.2H_2O = 561$

(Cambridge Open Schol.)

A21 Molar Reacting Weights (***)

Standardise the potassium permanganate (manganate(VII)) solution CA against the ammonium iron(II) sulphate solution CB.

(i) CC is a neutral solution of manganese(II) sulphate. Take 25 cm^3 of CC, dilute to roughly 100 cm^3 and add one specimen of the mixtures of 10 g $ZnSO_4$ and 1 g ZnO with which you are provided. Then heat to boiling. Titrate with CA at a temperature just below boiling-point until a pink colour remains on allowing the precipitate to settle. Then acidify with 1 cm^3 of glacial acetic (ethanoic) acid and complete the titration to a permanent pink.

(ii) Carry out *one* of your accurate titrations in a 250 cm^3 beaker and after the end-point is reached proceed as follows: Allow the precipitate to settle and decant the hot liquid through the sintered-glass funnel provided. Thoroughly wash the precipitate with water and decant and filter these washings but do *not* attempt to transfer the precipitate to the funnel. After completing the washings, place the sintered-glass funnel with the precipitate in the beaker and add 50 cm^3 of CB. Heat until all the precipitate has dissolved. Cool the solution and titrate with the manganate(VII) solution CA.

Write equations for the reactions which have occurred. Calculate the concentration of manganese(II) sulphate in CC from your results in (i) and check this answer with your result in part (ii).

(Cambridge Open Schol.)

A22 Molar Reacting Weights (**)

Solution CC1 contains $7 \cdot 00$ g dm^{-3} of ammonium vanadyl(IV) oxalate (ethanedioate) in which vanadium has the oxidation number of $+4$.

Caution. Oxalates (ethanedioates) are poisonous.

(a) Place your manganate(VII) solution ($0 \cdot 0200$ M or $3 \cdot 16$ g dm^{-3}) in the burette.

Take either 20 or 25 cm^3 of CC1 by pipette (with care, or use a pipette filler), add an equal volume of dilute sulphuric acid and heat the solution to 353–363 K. Titrate the hot solution with the manganate(VII) solution, maintaining the temperature above 333 K by reheating if necessary. A slight excess of manganate(VII) imparts a permanent pink coloration to the yellow solution. Use this solution in (b).

The oxalate (ethanedioate) has been destroyed and vanadium has been converted to the $+5$ oxidation state, thus:

$$2MnO_4^- + 5C_2O_4^{2-} + 16H^+ \rightarrow 2Mn^{2+} + 10CO_2 + 8H_2O$$

$$MnO_4^- + 8H^+ + 5VO^{2+} \rightarrow Mn^{2+} + 5VO^{3+} + 4H_2O$$

where

$$VO^{2+} = V^{4+} + O^{2-} \text{ and } VO^{3+} = V^{5+} + O^{2-}$$

(b) Add about 25 cm^3 of sodium sulphite (sulphate(IV)) solution but no more than that, to the residual solution from (a), and heat until reduction to blue vanadyl(IV) state is completed. Then boil the mixture gently for 600 s to expel the excess sulphur dioxide (IV oxide), allow to cool somewhat, and titrate with the permanganate (manganate(VII)) solution. Between 5 and 10 cm^3 of manganate(VII) should be required.

In this titration you have converted the vanadium from an oxidation state of $+4$ to one of $+5$.

Calculate the concentration of vanadium in CC1 in moles per cubic decimetre.

Calculate the concentration of oxalate in CC1 in moles per cubic decimetre.

The formula for the ammonium vanadyl(IV) oxalate is reputed to be $(NH_4)_2[VO(C_2O_4)_2]2H_2O$.

From your results deduce the molar ratio of $C_2O_4^{2-}$ to V^{4+} ion and state, with a reason, whether it is in accord with the formula quoted for the complex oxalate.

(N.I.)

A23 Molar Reacting Weights (*)

You are provided with:

a solution of sodium chloride containing 5·85 g dm^{-3}, labelled C;
a solution of silver(I) nitrate, labelled D;
a solution of the salt $MCl_2.xH_2O$ containing 10·95 g dm^{-3}, labelled E;
a suitable indicator.

(a) Titrate 25 cm^3 portions of C with D and hence obtain the molarity of D.

(b) Titrate 25 cm^3 portions of E with D and hence obtain the molar weight of $MCl_2.xH_2O$.

(c) Assuming that $MCl_2.xH_2O$ contains 49·3% of water of crystallisation, calculate the value of x.

(d) Calculate the atomic weight (relative atomic mass) of the metal M.

B1 Solubility (*)

You are asked to determine the solubility of the salt Z in water at various temperatures. Proceed as follows:

Weigh out 10·0 g of Z into a clean boiling-tube. From a burette, run into the tube 6 cm^3 of pure water. Heat the mixture of salt and water carefully in a bunsen flame until all the salt has dissolved, and the solution is quite clear. You will have to boil the solution *gently* to accomplish this.

Now allow the solution to cool, stirring it *gently* with the thermo-meter supplied. Cooling can be hastened by dipping the boiling-tube in and out of a beaker of cooler water.

Note the temperature at which crystals of solid first appear. Check this temperature by warming the tube until the crystals have again dissolved, and then repeating the cooling process.

Now add, from the burette, exactly 2 cm³ more of water and then repeat the above operations so as to find the temperature at which crystals appear. Add 2 cm³ more of water. Repeat the reading.

When you have made *four* successive additions of 2 cm³ of water, stop the experiment. You should now have five results.

Plot a graph showing saturation temperature against total volume of water present in the solution.

Using this curve, calculate the solubility of Z in water at 328 K.

Comment on the accuracy of this experiment for the determination of solubility.

(O. and C.)

B2 Solutions: Depression of the Freezing-point (*)

The freezing-point of a pure solvent is depressed by the addition of a non-volatile solute. If w_2 grammes of solute are dissolved in w_1 grammes of solvent, M is the molar weight (relative molecular mass) of the solute, K is the freezing constant (the depression which would be produced by dissolving 1 mole of solute in 1000 g of solvent) and t is the depression of the freezing-point observed, then it can be shown that

$$M = \frac{w_2 \times 1\,000 \times K}{w_1 \times t}$$

You are provided with a simple freezing-point apparatus as shown in the following sketch, and a solid X whose relative molecular mass is required.

(*a*) Into the tube A pour 25 cm³ of pure benzene (density 0·88 g cm⁻³), then replace A in the freezing-bath. Stir the crushed ice well and note the temperature (t_1) at which the benzene freezes. As soon as the freezing-point has been reached, remove A before the benzene has become wholly solid and allow the crystals to melt in air, noting the temperature (t_2) at which the crystals have all disappeared.

(*b*) Now weigh out between 500 and 700 mg of solid X, showing

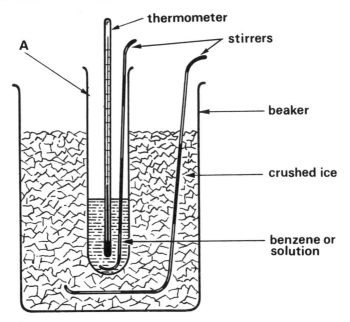

your weighings clearly. Add this to the benzene in A, shake it carefully until X has dissolved, and then replace A in the freezing-bath. Redetermine the two temperatures mentioned in (*a*), calling them t_3 and t_4, respectively.

(*c*) Redetermine the temperatures t_3 and t_4 using an accurately known weight of X lying between 1 000 and 1 200 mg.

(*d*) The depression of the freezing-point is given by $(t_1 - t_3)$ and $(t_2 - t_4)$, this helping to eliminate supercooling errors if you take the average.

For each of your sets of results, determine the molar weight of X and quote the average value as your true value for this quantity.

Comment on the accuracy of this experiment. How would you attempt to improve it?

The freezing constant for benzene is 5·12 K per 1 000 g.

B3 Solutions: Depression of the Freezing-point (*)

The theory of this experiment is given in experiment B2. In the present experiment, the solvent used is liquid camphor which has an unusually high freezing constant. Thus, large depressions of the freezing- (melting-) point occur even with small amounts of solute.

(a) Weigh out by a difference method (to 3 places of decimals) about 2 g of finely powdered camphor in a small dry test-tube. Now add about 100 mg of solid X provided and find the weight of the latter. Hold the tube with a piece of folded paper and warm it carefully over a small bunsen flame until you have a liquid present, and insert the bulb of the thermometer into the liquid using a small piece of rubber tubing provided to secure the thermometer in the tube.

Allow the liquid to cool and solidify and then clamp the test-tube as shown in a beaker of liquid paraffin. Heat the oil-bath over a medium bunsen flame using a tripod and gauze, keeping the oil well stirred. Heat much more gently above 403 K. The mixture will melt first to a milky liquid and you should note the temperature at which this liquid becomes clear, which is the melting-point of the mixture.

(b) Using the *same* thermometer but a different test-tube, find the melting-point of pure camphor in the same way.

Record all weighings and, if possible, repeat the determination (a) using different proportions of camphor and X.

From your results, calculate the molar weight of X. The freezing-point of camphor is 40·0 K per 1 000 g.

B4 Solubility and Solubility Product (***)

Ethylenediamine tetra-acetic acid (E.D.T.A.) forms a stable water-soluble complex with most metallic ions carrying two or more positive charges and is a sensitive reagent for the determination of low concentrations of such ions. Here the reaction is being used for the determination of the solubility of the sparingly soluble copper(II) benzoate (benzenecarboxylate) salt. E.D.T.A. is used in the form of its disodium salt and one mole of this reacts with one mole of copper(II) ions in alkaline solution.

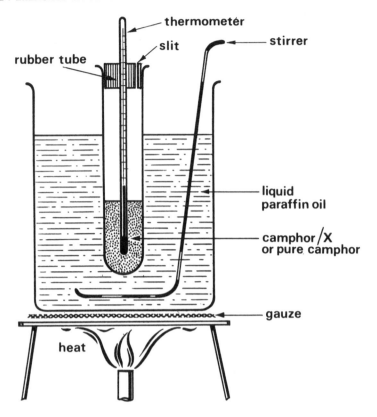

HA is a solution of copper(II) sulphate in water.

HB is a solution of sodium benzoate (benzenecarboxylate) in water.

HC is a buffer solution of ammonium chloride/ammonia solution in water.

HD are 'murexide' indicator tablets.

HE is a solution of the disodium salt of E.D.T.A. in water.

The exact concentrations of solutions HA and HB will be given to you by your teacher and will be quoted in mole dm^{-3}.

(a) *Preparation of a saturated solution of copper(II) benzoate*

Take a clean, dry conical flask and pipette into it 40 cm^3 of solution HA and 40 cm^3 of solution HB. Shake the flask to mix the solutions thoroughly and note the time. Prepare a second flask in exactly the same way and allow both flasks to stand for one hour before proceeding as instructed in (c) below.

The number of benzoate ions (C_6H_5COO) in solution HB exceeds that needed to combine with all the copper(II) ions (Cu^{2+}) in solution HA.

Calculate the concentration in mole dm^{-3} of the excess benzoate ions in the solution obtained on mixing solutions HA and HB.

(b) *Standardisation of HE (a solution of the disodium salt of E.D.T.A.)*

Take a conical flask and pipette into it 20 cm^3 of a solution of HA, then from a measuring cylinder add about 40 cm^3 of distilled water. Shake the contents of the flask and add the buffer solution HC drop by drop until the pale blue precipitate which first forms just redissolves to form a royal blue solution. Add one indicator tablet HD, crush it with a glass rod and shake the contents of the flask. Titrate with HE; the apple green colour fades gradually to an indefinite colour and then changes suddenly to a bright mauve colour at the end-point. Repeat the procedure until two consistent titres are obtained. From your results, calculate the concentration in mole dm^{-3} of disodium E.D.T.A. in solution HE.

(1 mole $CuSO_4$ = 1 mole disodium E.D.T.A.)

(c) *Determination of the copper(II) ion concentration in the saturated solution of copper(II) benzoate (benzenecarboxylate)*

After it has been standing for one hour, take one of the flasks prepared in (a) above and measure the temperature of the solution. Some of the copper(II) benzoate will have been precipitated leaving a saturated solution. Filter the contents of the flask (using a fine-porosity paper) into a clean, dry conical flask or beaker but do not wash the precipitate. Pipette a 40 cm^3 portion of the filtrate into another conical flask, add the buffer solution HC drop by drop until the pale blue precipitate which first forms just redissolves to give a royal blue solution, add one indicator tablet HD and titrate with HE as described in (b). Repeat the whole procedure with the contents of the second flask prepared in (a). Take the mean of the two titres and calculate the concentration in mole dm^{-3} of copper (II) ions remaining in solution.

(d) Calculate the solubility product of copper(II) benzoate

(remember the excess benzoate ions) and from this the solubility of the anhydrous salt in water in g dm^{-3}.

(Formula weight of copper(II) benzoate = 306.)

Set out your results like this:

Concentration of copper(II) sulphate
in solution HA   .... mole dm^{-3}
Concentration of sodium benzoate
in solution HB   .... mole dm^{-3}

(a) *Preparation of a saturated solution of copper(II) benzoate*

Concentration of excess benzoate ions
after mixing HA/HB   .... mole dm^{-3}

(b) *Standardisation of HE (a solution of the disodium salt of E.D.T.A.)*

Final level
Initial level
Titre   Mean titre.............. cm^3
Concentration of the disodium salt
of E.D.T.A.   .... mole dm^{-3}

(c) *Determination of copper(II) ion concentration in the saturated solution of copper(II) benzoate*

Final temperature   Flask 1........K   Flask 2........K
Final level
Initial level
Titre   Mean titre............. cm^3
Concentration of copper(II) ions
remaining in solution   .... mole dm^{-3}

(d) *Calculation of solubility product and of solubility*

Solubility product of copper(II) benzoate   ....
Solubility of copper(II) benzoate in water   .... g dm^{-3}
                                     (O. and C.)

B5 Phase Equilibria (*)

You are given eight boiling-tubes, loosely stoppered, containing mixtures of the substances A and B in various proportions.

Tube	Grammes A	Grammes B	Temperature for beginning of freezing
1	5·0	0·0	
2	4·0	1·0	
3	3·3	1·7	
4	3·0	2·0	
5	2·0	3·0	
6	1·7	3·3	
7	1·0	4·0	
8	0·0	5·0	

Put some water into a tall beaker, bring it to the boil, and then use the two rubber bands provided to form a bundle of the eight tubes. When the water is boiling gently, put in the bundle of tubes and stir the tubes round until the contents melt. Remove the flame, place the thermometer in the water, and stand the beaker on an asbestos pad on the bench.

As the temperature falls, every few degrees remove the tubes and shake from side to side until crystallisation just begins in one of them. Replace the tube in the water-bath; if the number of crystals is seen to decrease the temperature is still too high (judge *how* high by the rate of dissolving); if the crystals form very rapidly after replacing the tube, the temperature is too low. The making of this measurement is very sensitive if only a few tiny crystals are present.

In your table, record the temperature at which crystallisation just starts. As you deal with each tube, remove it from the bundle and place it in a stock beaker.

When the temperature has fallen to 323 K, the cooling of the water becomes too slow and you should hasten this process by adding small volumes of cold water; you should not lower the temperature by more than one degree per addition.

When the temperature has fallen to 313 K, the tubes will not cool sufficiently rapidly in the air to start crystallisation before replacing in the water-bath, and in order to obtain readings here you should try dipping the tubes for an instant in a cold water bath.

Plot a graph to represent the temperature of freezing (ordinate axis) against the percentage composition (abscissa axis). Make an estimate of any probable sources of error in your readings. Comment on any special features of the graph you notice.

B6 Mutual Solubilities (**)

Three-quarters fill a large beaker with tap water and heat it to about 343 K. While it is heating, weigh out 5 g ($\pm$0·1 g) of solid A into a clean dry boiling-tube and add to it 2 cm^3 of purified water from a burette. N.B. Solid A is corrosive and should not be handled. Rest the boiling-tube in the beaker of warm water, stirring the contents of the tube *gently* with the thermometer. Note the temperature at which the liquid in the tube becomes clear. By moving the tube in and out of the hot water bath, stirring continuously, take a number of readings of the temperature at which (a) the cooling liquid goes turbid ('milky') and (b) the heated liquid goes clear again. The mean of these temperatures gives the miscibility temperature for this mixture. To save time, cooling under the tap is recommended for the first reading.

Now add another 1 cm^3 of purified water to the mixture already in the boiling-tube and repeat the above operations to determine the miscibility temperature of this new mixture. Continue adding 1 cm^3 portions of water until a total of 6 cm^3 of water have been added, and thereafter add 2 cm^3 portions of water at a time until a total of 20 cm^3 of water have been added, determining the miscibility temperature after each addition.

Record your observations in a table as follows and, assuming that 1 cm^3 of water weighs 1 g, calculate the percentage by weight of A present in each mixture (column 3).

Draw a graph of your results, plotting temperature of miscibility against percentage composition of A by weight, carefully labelling your axes.

What conclusions (if any) can you draw from your results?

Use your diagram to explain what will happen if a mixture consisting of 5 g of A and 5 g of water is heated to (a) 328 K, (b) 348 K.

Weight of A (in g)	Weight of water (in g)	Weight % of A in mixture	Miscibility temperature on heating t_1	on cooling t_2	mean $\dfrac{t_1+t_2}{2}$
5	2				
5	3				
etc.	etc.				

B7 Partition (Distribution) Law (***)

HA   is a standard solution of sodium hydroxide in water.
The exact molarity will be given by your teacher.

HB   is an aqueous solution of phenoxyacetic (ethanoic) acid,
$$C_6H_5OCH_2COOH.$$

HC   is carbon tetrachloride (tetrachloromethane).

HD   is chloroform (trichloromethane).

(a) Determine the molar concentration of phenoxyacetic acid as follows. Using a pipette or a burette, measure out 10 cm³ of solution HB into a conical flask and titrate against the sodium hydroxide solution HA, using phenolphthalein as indicator.

Repeat this procedure until two consistent titres are obtained. From your results, calculate the molarity of the phenoxyacetic acid solution HB.

(b) Examine the distribution of phenoxyacetic acid between carbon tetrachloride (tetrachloromethane) and water as follows. Using a pipette or a burette, measure out 40 cm³ of solution HB into a conical flask (or a bottle), then add 40 cm³ of carbon tetrachloride (HC) *from a burette*. Insert the stopper, shake the flask for about 60 s, allow the flask to stand for 300 s and take the temperature of the liquid. Then, tilt the flask and *using the safety attachment provided*, transfer 10 cm³ of the upper (aqueous) layer to another conical flask and titrate the phenoxyacetic acid against sodium hydroxide using phenolphthalein as indicator. Repeat the procedure until two consistent titres are obtained. If more than *three* titrations are required, repeat the whole of procedure (*b*).

Calculate the molar concentration of phenoxyacetic acid remaining in the aqueous layer and, by subtraction, deduce the molar concentration of phenoxyacetic acid in the carbon tetrachloride layer. Then, calculate the distribution constant from the following expression:

$$D = \frac{(\text{molarity of phenoxyacetic acid in } CCl_4 \text{ layer})^{\frac{1}{2}}}{\text{molarity of phenoxyacetic acid in aqueous layer}}$$

(*c*) Examine the distribution of phenoxyacetic acid between chloroform and water as follows. Using a pipette or a burette, measure out 40 cm^3 of solution HB into a conical flask (or bottle) then add 10 cm^3 of chloroform (HD) from a burette. Insert the stopper, shake the flask for about 60 s, allow the flask to stand for 300 s and take the temperature of the liquid. Then titrate 10 cm^3 portions of the aqueous layer as in (*b*) above.

Calculate the molar concentration of phenoxyacetic acid remaining in the aqueous layer and, by subtraction, deduce the molar concentration of phenoxyacetic acid in the chloroform layer. Then calculate the distribution constant from the following expression:

$$D' = \frac{(\text{molarity of phenoxyacetic acid in } CHCl_3 \text{ layer})^{\frac{1}{2}}}{\text{molarity of phenoxyacetic acid in aqueous layer}}$$

(*d*) Comment on the difference between the distribution constants you have determined.

Set out your results like this:

Molarity of Solution HA . . . .

(*a*) *Standardisation of solution HB*

Final level
Initial level
Titre   Mean titre . . . . cm^3
                              Molarity of solution HB . . . .

(*b*) *Distribution of phenoxyacetic acid between CCl$_4$ and water*

Temperature . . . . K

Final level
Initial level
Titre   Mean titre . . . . cm^3

Molarity of phenoxyacetic acid in
   aqueous layer   ....(m_1)
Molarity of phenoxyacetic acid in CCl_4
   layer   ....(m_2)
Distribution constant $= \sqrt{m_2}/m_1$ .... (D)

(c) *Distribution of phenoxyacetic acid between $CHCl_3$ and water*

                            Temperature.......... K

Final level
Initial level
Titre   Mean titre........ cm^3
   Molarity of phenoxyacetic acid in
      aqueous layer   ....(m_3)
   Molarity of phenoxyacetic acid in
      $CHCl_3$ layer   ....(m_4)
   Distribution constant $= \sqrt{m_4}/m_3$ .... (D')

(d) *Comment on the difference between the distribution constants D and D'*

                                 (O. and C.)

B8 Partition (Distribution) Law (**)

The object of this experiment is to determine the value of n in the formula of the complex formed when ammonia is added to copper(II) ions in aqueous solution.

$$Cu^{2+}(aq) + n\,NH_3(aq) \rightleftharpoons Cu(NH_3)_n^{2+}(aq)$$

(*a*) Standardise the given aqueous solution of ammonia using 0·2 M sulphuric acid with methyl red as indicator, the acid being put in the burette.

(*b*) Determine the partition coefficient (distribution constant) for ammonia between water and chloroform (trichloromethane). In a dry stoppered bottle put 50·00 cm^3 of chloroform, using a pipette filler. Then add 5·00 cm^3 of aqueous ammonia.

  * Shake vigorously, stand for a moment, swirl and stand for about 300 s.

In a second stoppered bottle place approximately 200 cm³ of distilled water. Using a 20·00 cm³ pipette, extract 20·00 cm³ of chloroform from the first bottle and transfer it to the 200 cm³ of water in the second bottle. Remember to poke the pipette straight down into the chloroform layer and try to avoid getting a globule of water in the pipette.

Stopper the bottle, shake well, stand for a moment, swirl and then stand for about 300 s. Now, using the same pipette, you can remove most of the chloroform (which has now had most of the ammonia removed from it) with the minimum of aqueous layer and reject it.

To the aqueous layer left, add several drops of methyl red and titrate the whole bottle full with 0·0 1M sulphuric acid. From this result you will obtain the amount of ammonia in 20·00 cm³ of chloroform layer.

Use this to calculate the number of millimoles of ammonia in 50·00 cm³ of chloroform layer.

1 cm³ of 0·01 M sulphuric acid ≡ 0·02 mmol ammonia.

Calculate the number of millimoles of ammonia there were in the original 5·00 cm³ and, by subtraction, obtain the number of millimoles of ammonia left in the aqueous layer.

$$\text{Partition coefficient} = \frac{\text{concn of ammonia in aqueous layer}}{\text{concn of ammonia in chloroform}}$$

$$= \frac{\text{moles ammonia (aq)} \div \text{vol aq}}{\text{moles ammonia } (CHCl_3) \div \text{vol } CHCl_3}$$

$$= \frac{\text{moles ammonia (aq)}}{\text{moles ammonia } (CHCl_3)} \times \frac{\text{vol } CHCl_3}{\text{vol aq}}$$

Note: moles of ammonia (aq) means the total number of moles of ammonia in that particular volume of water.

(c) Determine n. Wash the first stoppered bottle and 20·00 cm³ pipette with a little acetone (propanone) and blow dry in air. Mix 50·00 cm³ of chloroform, 5·00 cm³ of 0·05 M aqueous copper(II) sulphate, 2·00 cm³ aqueous ammonia in a stoppered bottle and treat this as in (b) above from the asterisk (*) onwards. Then

$$\text{moles ammonia (aq)} =$$

$$\text{moles ammonia } (CHCl_3) \times \frac{\text{vol aq}}{\text{vol } CHCl_3} \times \text{part. coeff.}$$

From this you can calculate (i) the number of millimoles of ammonia in all the chloroform layer and hence (ii) the number of millimoles of free ammonia in the aqueous layer, (iii) the ammonia bound to the copper(II) ion, i.e. the ammonia at the start in 2 cm^3 minus the ammonia free in the aqueous layer minus the ammonia in the chloroform, (iv) the ratio of ammonia to copper(II) ions in the complex.

What is the structure of the complex ion?

B9   Partition (Distribution) Law: Ionic Theory (***)

The idea of this experiment is to determine the hydrolysis constant K_h of the salt phenylammonium chloride, using a partition method.

$$K_h = \frac{[\text{aniline}][\text{acid}]}{[\text{salt}]}$$

(a) Determine the partition coefficient of aniline (aminobenzene) between water and carbon tetrachloride (tetrachloromethane) as follows.

Dissolve approximately 0·3 cm^3 of aniline in 30 cm^3 of carbon tetrachloride in a stoppered bottle, add 150 cm^3 of distilled water, and shake at laboratory temperature for about 1·8 ks.

Titrate 50 cm^3 portions of the aqueous layer and 10 cm^3 portions of the organic layer as follows. Add about 10 cm^3 of 15% hydrochloric acid to each portion and run in, from a burette, a measured volume of X (containing 0·0167 M potassium bromate(V) and 0·1 M potassium bromide). The volume added should be just in excess of that required to convert the aniline to its 2,4,6-tribromo-derivative. This is shown by the appearance of yellow free bromine.

$$HBrO_3 + 5HBr \rightarrow 3Br_2 + 3H_2O$$

2,4,6 − tribromoaniline

Determine the excess added by adding 5 cm of 0·25 M potassium iodide solution and then titrating the iodine released with 0·1 M sodium thiosulphate solution (Y).

Before titration of the organic layer, add approximately 30 cm^3 of distilled water.

(b) Now shake 100 cm^3 of solution Z (phenylammonium chloride solution containing 8·0 g of the salt in 500 cm^3 of water) with 100 cm^3 of carbon tetrachloride, as before. Titrate 25 cm^3 portions of the organic layer as described in (a).

(c) Calculate and write down the partition coefficient.

(d) Using this value, determine the concentration of free aniline in the aqueous layer when the phenylammonium chloride was used.

(e) The total free aniline in both layers is equal to the concentration of H_3O^+ ions in the aqueous layer. The concentration of salt not hydrolysed can thus be found, by difference, giving the concentration of phenylammonium ions.

(f) Finally calculate the value of K_h and write down this value for inspection.

B10 Partition (Distribution) Law (**)

You are supplied with:
An aqueous solution of acetic (ethanoic) acid, labelled A
2-methylpropan-1-ol (isobutyl alcohol), labelled B
1 M sodium hydroxide, labelled C.

Determine by the following method the distribution coefficient of acetic (ethanoic) acid between water and 2-methylpropan-1-ol.

Using a measuring cylinder, measure into a 250 cm^3 separating funnel, 100 cm^3 of aqueous acetic acid and 60 cm^3 of 2-methylpropan 1-ol. Shake the mixture for at least 120 s and then allow the two layers to separate. Run off some of the lower (aqueous) layer into a burette and measure out 25 cm^3 into a conical flask. Titrate with 1 M sodium hydroxide solution using phenolphalein as indicator. Repeat with a second 25 cm^3 portion of the aqueous layer. Add the alcoholic layer to the burette and complete the separation of the aqueous layer. Measure out 25 cm^3 of the alcoholic layer and titrate as before. Repeat with a second 25 cm^3 portion of the alcoholic layer.

Calculate the distribution coefficient (water/alcohol) of the acetic acid.

Give a qualitative estimate of the magnitude of the error which would result from an incomplete separation of the two layers, i.e. traces of one layer present in the other.

(A.E.B.)

B11   Ionic Theory (**)

The following equilibrium exists in a solution of a weak acid, HA.

$$HA \leftrightharpoons H^+ + A^-$$

and so

$$H^+ = K \frac{[HA]}{[A^-]}$$

$$= K \frac{[acid]}{[salt]}$$

where K is the dissociation constant of the acid and the square brackets represent concentrations in moles per cubic decimetre.

We assume that all the anions A$^-$ arise from dissociation of the highly dissociated salt.

The object of this experiment is to compare the dissociation constants of acetic (ethanoic) and lactic (2-hydroxypropanoic) acids.

You are provided with solution HA$_1$ (acetic acid) and HA$_2$ (lactic acid). Determine the molarity of each by titration with the solution HA_3 provided, which is standard 0.1 M sodium hydroxide. Use phenolphthalein as indicator and set out your results in the form of a table.

In five boiling-tubes, labelled X 1, 2, 4, 6, 8 prepare mixtures containing 10 cm^3 of the weaker acid, acetic, and 1, 2, 4, 6, 8 cm^3 of 0.1 M sodium hydroxide solution HA_3, respectively. Add 4 drops of bromophenol blue indicator to each tube, shake carefully, and examine the colour.

Label a second set of tubes Y 1, 2, 4, 6, 8 and add to each 5 cm^3 of the stronger acid (lactic). Add indicator as before and titrate the acid in each tube with 0.1 M sodium hydroxide, HA_3, until the colour of the indicator matches as nearly as possible that in the corresponding series X tube.

When this is so, we see that

$$K_A M_A = K_L M_L$$

where K is the dissociation constant, M the molar ratio of acid to salt, and A and L refer to acetic and lactic acids, respectively. From your results, calculate the average ratio of K_A to K_L, explaining clearly the stages in your calculation.

B12   Solutions: Paper Chromatography (*)

You are provided with two substances:

A   made by powdering dried leaves from an herbaceous plant.
B   made by powdering leaves (red/brown) of a tree.

(*a*) To the tube containing A add approximately 5 cm^3 of acetone (propanone) and heat the mixture in a beaker of boiling water until you have obtained a solution of the pigments. Filter the solution, collecting the filtrate in a watch-glass. With the aid of the small capillary tube provided, put one tiny drop of the concentrated solution at spot X on the filter paper strip, as shown in the diagram. Allow the spot to dry and then repeat the procedure several times until a really concentrated (but small) spot is present.

Using a bent pin, attach the strip of paper to the cork as shown, and adjust the length until the strip almost reaches the bottom of the tube. The width of the strip must be such that it does not touch the sides of the tube. Remove the paper strip and cork from the tube and put in a depth of 10 mm of solvent S. *This solvent is highly inflammable.* Replace the cork and paper and leave it, set upright in a test-tube rack, until the solvent has almost reached the top of the paper. Then remove the paper and allow it to dry in air, after first marking the position reached by the ascending solvent.

(*b*) Repeat the whole process for B.

(*c*) Stick both dry paper strips to your answer sheet. What information about substances A and B can you obtain from the strips? Why has solvent S produce the patterns shown?

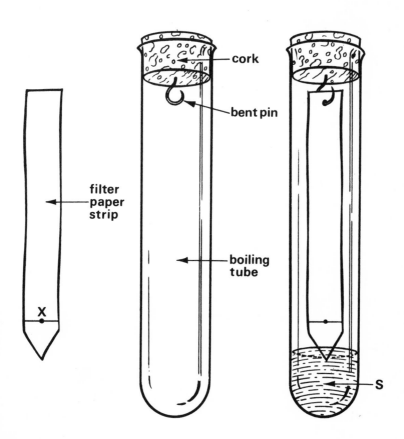

Measure and record the migrations of all separated components of A and B, relative to the solvent front (the R_f values).

B13 Solutions: Paper Chromatography (*)

You are provided with aqueous solutions of three salts, A, B and C, all of which are nitrates. For this experiment you will require to use ascending paper chromatography apparatus as described for experiment B 12.

(*a*) Put a tiny spot of each solution at X on the base-line drawn on the strip of filter paper, allowing each spot to dry before another is applied. Continue in this way until three spots of each solution have been applied.

(*b*) Develop the chromatogram using distilled water as the solvent S.

(*c*) When the solvent front has almost reached the top of the paper, remove the paper, mark the solvent front, and allow the paper to dry in air.

Then dip the paper into the potassium chromate(VI) solution provided, and wash away the surplus reagent with water.

(*d*) Allow the paper to dry throughly and then measure the migration of each component relative to the distance travelled by the solvent front. This is called the R_f value. Record the three R_f values on your answer paper.

B14 Solutions: Thin-layer Chromatography (*)

Thin-layer chromatography can be applied to all problems to which paper chromatography can be applied. In this experiment you are provided with a mixture of some transition metal cations which you are required to separate and then measure the R_f values (the distance migrated relative to the solvent front).

You are provided with thin-layer plates (or 'chromatoplates') coated with silica gel. Spot a sample of the solution X provided,

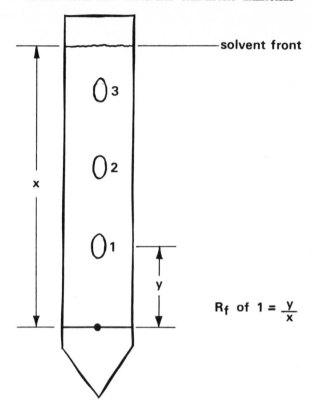

$$R_f \text{ of } 1 = \frac{y}{x}$$

which contains cobalt(II), iron(III), manganese(II) and nickel(II
ions, on to a base-line on the thin-layer plate, making sure that the
diameter of the spot you apply is not too large (2 mm diameter
maximum, if possible).

Allow the spot to dry and then reapply the solution, and repeat
this procedure until four such spots have been applied to the same
point on the base-line.

Allow the dried plate to stand in a beaker (or gas jar) containing
solvent Y until the solvent front has almost reached the top of the
plate.

Remove the plate and allow the solvent to evaporate. Then expose
the plate to ammonia vapour—hold the plate over a beaker containing concentrated ammonia solution (*care*) in the fume chamber.

Immediately spray the plate with locating reagent Z. Record the colours of the complexes formed and the R_f values of the components.

Component number	Colour of complex	R_f Value
1		
2		
3		
4		

When the plate is dry, over-spray it with the fixing spray provided and attach it to your answer paper by means of Sellotape. Comment on the factors which aid separation of components in thin-layer chromatography. Why can it be more useful than paper chromatography?

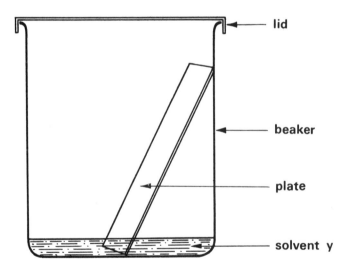

C1 Chemical Kinetics (*)

The idea of this experiment is to study the decomposition of hydrogen peroxide solution in the presence of manganese(IV) oxide as catalyst.

$$2H_2O_2 \rightarrow 2H_2O + O_2$$

You are provided with the following solutions:

HA_1 6-volume aqueous hydrogen peroxide.

HA_2 borate buffer solution.

HA_3 0·01 M potassium permanganate (manganate(VII)) solution.

Into the conical flask provided place 10 cm³ of the solution HA_1 and 50 cm³ of HA_2 and mix them thoroughly by swirling. Arrange the flask by clamping it in a bowl of water at 293 K—adjust the temperature of this by addition of hot or cold water from the stock supplies. Record the temperature of the bowl of water.

Meanwhile, fill the burette with HA_3.

While swirling the flask, pipette in 5 cm³ of solution HA_3 *rapidly* (blow it out) and ensure that the contents of the flask are mixed *thoroughly*; then restore the flask to the bowl. Have one or two clean conical flasks ready for sampling and have 15 cm³ of bench dilute sulphuric acid ready in each one. Note a convenient time on your stop-clock and take a 10 cm³ sample from the flask, calling the time t_0 as the sample is put in the titration flask. After the sample has been placed in the sulphuric acid, the manganese(IV) oxide catalyst is destroyed and no further reaction takes place (further decomposition is very slow). Titrate with HA_3 to a pale pink end-point.

After intervals of 300 s, 600 s, 900 s and 1·2 ks, and so on, repeat the sampling and titration and continue up to 3·6 ks.

Set out your results in tabular form, then plot a graph of titre against time, i.e. cm³ against s. From the graph, make several determinations of the 'half-life' period of the reaction. Comment on your results, and determine the order of reaction. Why is it unnecessary to know the molarity of the hydrogen peroxide? Comment on the accuracy of this experiment, pointing out probable sources of error.

Explain how the catalyst is formed in this reaction.

C2   Chemical Kinetics (***)

You are provided with the following solutions:

HA   is a solution of iodine (0·02 M) in potassium iodide solution (0·2 M).

HB   is an aqueous solution of acetone (propanone) (1·0 M).
HC   is sulphuric acid (1·0 M).
HD   is sodium hydrogen carbonate solution (0·5 M).
HE   is sodium thiosulphate (0·01 M).

The iodination of acetone (propanone) is catalysed by hydrogen ions in aqueous solution and proceeds at a rate which is directly proportional to the concentration of acetone. The way in which the rate of reaction depends on the iodine concentration can be determined by using a large excess of acetone, so that its concentration is virtually unaltered during the reaction. Perform the following exercises.

(a) In a conical flask, labelled 1, place 50 cm^3 HA$_3$, and in a second flask, labelled 2, place 25 cm^3 HB and 25 cm^3 HC.

(b) Into each of several conical flasks (labelled 3, 4, 5, 6, etc.) place 10 cm^3 portions of HD.

(c) Carefully, noting the time, pour the contents of 2 into 1 and shake well for 60 s. Then, noting the time, withdraw 10 cm^3 of the reaction mixture, run this *rapidly* into 3, shake until bubbling ceases (of what?) and titrate the residual iodine with HE.

(d) At measured and noted intervals, from 300 to 600 s, repeat operation (c) using flasks 4, 5, 6, etc. Do not continue past 3·6 ks.

(e) Present your results in tabular form and draw a graph of the residual iodine against the time of reaction. Comment on your results and indicate the probable dependance of the reaction rate upon the iodine concentration.

Record the temperature of your reaction mixture in 1 at the start and finish of the experiment (why?).

Provided the solutions are at the stated concentrations, 1 cm^3 of reaction mixture is equivalent to 2 cm^3 of 0·01 M sodium thiosulphate.

C3   Chemical Kinetics (**)

The reaction featured in this experiment involves the interaction of hydrogen peroxide and hydrogen iodide in aqueous solution.

$$H_2O_2 + 2HI \rightarrow 2H_2O + I_2$$

From the equation, it appears that the rate is directly proportional to the concentration of the hydrogen peroxide and to the square of the concentration of hydriodic acid; but in the presence of sodium thiosulphate, iodine formed is converted immediately to hydriodic acid and the concentration of this remains constant.

Into the large flask provided, put 800 cm^3 distilled water, 25 cm^3 of 1 M sulphuric acid, and a few cm^3 of starch solution.

Fill a burette with 0·1 M sodium thiosulphate solution.

Add the potassium iodide solution (X) to the flask and run in 2 cm^3 of the thiosulphate. Then add 4 cm^3 of 10 volume hydrogen peroxide solution. Start your stop-clock when half the hydrogen peroxide has been added and record the time when a deep blue colour appears. Then quickly add a further 2 cm^3 of thiosulphate, swirl the flask and its contents, and note the time when the blue colour reappears. Continue in this way until ten readings have been obtained.

Determine the concentration of the hydrogen peroxide solution by first diluting it ten times (accurately) and then titrating with 0·02 M potassium permanganate (manganate(VII)) solution. Remember to add dilute sulphuric acid before titrating.

The amount of hydrogen peroxide present initially can be deduced from your titration results, and the amount used up after a time t is directly proportional to the volume of thiosulphate run into the flask.

If m cm^3 of thiosulphate is equivalent to the initial volume of hydrogen peroxide, m is directly proportional to a, the initial molar concentration, in the kinetic equation for the reaction.

$$t = 2 \cdot 3 \log_{10} \left[\frac{a}{a-x} \right]$$

In this equation, k is the rate constant and x is the number of moles of hydrogen peroxide removed after a time t seconds. Suppose n cm^3 of thiosulphate have been added after t seconds, then $(m-n)$ is directly proportional to $(a-x)$.

Draw up a table showing values of $(m-n)$ for measured values of t and plot a suitable straight-line graph which will demonstrate that the reaction is first order. From this line, deduce the value (with correct units) of the rate constant, k. What factor must remain constant during the experiment, and why?

C4 Chemical Kinetics (***)

Determine the catalytic effect of iron(II) ions on the reaction

$$2I^- + S_2O_8^{2-} \rightarrow I_2 + 2SO_4^{2-}$$

by measuring the apparent reaction rate constant, k, in the absence and the presence of iron(II) ions.

With constant iodide ion concentration, the reaction is first order with respect to the persulphate ion concentration and the concentration of persulphate ions, c, at a time t is given by

$$\log_{10}\left[\frac{c_0}{c}\right] = \frac{kt}{2\cdot3}$$

where c_0 is the initial concentration of persulphate ions. The time taken for a known fraction of persulphate ions to react can therefore be used to determine k.

In the following instructions, the quantities refer to 25 cm³ pipettes; if you are using 20 cm³ pipettes, use the amounts shown in brackets.

HA   is a solution of potassium iodide, approximately 0·5 M.
HB   is a solution of potassium persulphate (peroxydisulphate), $K_2S_2O_8$.
HC   is a solution of sodium thiosulphate ($Na_2S_2O_3$), approximately 0·025 M.

(a) Determine the amount of persulphate, expressed as the equivalent number of cm³ of solution HC, V_0, in 25 cm³ (20 cm³) of solution HB as follows:

Put 50 cm³ (40 cm³) of HA plus 25 cm³ (20 cm³) of HB in a conical flask, heat to 323–328 K, and maintain at this temperature for 300 s to complete reaction. Place the flask on a white surface and titrate, at 323–328 K, with solution HC from a burette. Record your titre. *Only one titration is needed.*

(b) Determination of k in the absence of iron(II) ions at room temperature:

Means the time taken for a *quarter* of the initial concentration of persulphate ions to react, as follows. Prepare solutions in two flasks labelled A and B.

Flask A, 50 cm³ (60 cm³) of HA *plus* 25 cm³ (20 cm³) of distilled water *plus* a few drops of starch solution.

Flask B, 25 cm^3 (20 cm^3) of HB *plus* 50 cm^3 (40 cm^3) of distilled water.

From a burette add $\frac{1}{4}$ V$_0$ cm^3 of solution HC to flask B. *Noting the time*, pour the contents of flask A into flask B and mix thoroughly. Place the flask on a white surface and observe closely. Measure the temperature of the solution. Record the time of mixing and the temperature. Note, and record, the time, $t_{\frac{1}{4}}$, when the solution turns blue, which occurs when a *quarter* of the initial persulphate ions has reacted. Calculate *k* from your result.

(*c*) Determination of k in the presence of iron(II) ions at room temperature:

Prepare the same solutions in flask A and B as in (*b*) after washing out the flasks thoroughly. Add 5 cm^3 of 0.005 M iron(II) ion solution to flask A and, from a burette, $\frac{1}{2}$V$_0$ cm^3 of HC to flask B. Determine the time taken for *half* the initial persulphate ions to react. Calculate k from your results.

(*d*) Calculate the ratio

$$\frac{k \text{ (in presence of actalyst)}}{k \text{ (in absence of catalyst)}}$$

Set out your results like this:

Volume of pipette used........ cm^3

(*a*) Determination of amount of persulphate in 25 cm^3 (20 cm^3) of solution HB, expressed as equivalent number of cm^3 of solution HC.

Titre, V$_0$........ cm^3

(*b*) Temperature of solution ....K
Time of mixing ....
Time of appearance of blue colour ....

$t_{\frac{1}{4}}$.............

    k (in absence of catalyst) ....

(*c*) Temperature of solution ....K
Time of mixing ....
Time of appearance of blue colour ....

$t_{\frac{1}{2}}$.............

    k (in presence of catalyst) ....

(*d*) ratio $\dfrac{k \text{ (in presence of catalyst)}}{k \text{ (in absence of catalyst)}}$ ....

(O. and C.)

C5   Chemical Kinetics (**)

The acid-catalysed hydrolysis of the ester methyl acetate (ethanoate) can be represented by the equation:

$$CH_3COOCH_3(aq) + H_2O(l) \rightleftharpoons CH_3COOH(aq) + CH_3OH(aq)$$

You are provided with the following:

HA   1·0 M hydrochloric acid in a stoppered flask.
HB   0·50 M sodium hydroxide solution.
HC   methyl acetate (ethanoate) in a stoppered flask.

The flasks containing the acid and the ester have been clamped in a bath containing water at 313 K for several kiloseconds so that they have attained this temperature.

Add the ester to the acid and swirl gently and thoroughly so that the reactants become mixed. Start the stop-clock and replace the flask containing the reaction mixture in the bath at 313 K. After about 180 s, withdraw 10 cm^3 of the mixture by means of a pipette provided and run it into 50 cm^3 of distilled water, recording the time when the pipette is half empty. *Immediately* titrate the reaction mixture with HB, using phenolphthalein. Repeat the sampling procedure at about 300 s intervals, continuing up to 3·6 ks. In each case pour the sample into 50 cm^3 of water and titrate with HB.

Retain the remainder of your reaction mixture for a further 3·6 ks and then titrate at least two 10 cm^3 samples as described above, thus finding the acetic (ethanoic) acid produced after the reaction has proceeded as far as it will go. Let this final titre be V_{infin} and let the titre after a time t seconds be V_t. Since the concentration of hydrochloric acid catalyst remains constant throughout, V_{infin} gives a measure of the catalytic acid and the acetic (ethanoic) acid produced by complete hydrolysis. Hence, $(V_{infin} - V_t)$ gives a measure of the concentration of ester in the reaction mixture after a time t.

Tabulate your results of $(V_{infin} - V_t)$, $\log_{10}(V_{infin} - V_t)$ and t, and plot a graph of $\log_{10}(V_{infin} - V_t)$ as ordinate against t as abscissa. What is the order of the reaction? Read off the slope of the graph and, from this, deduce the value of the rate (velocity) constant for this reaction. Make sure that you give your answer with the correct units.

C6   Chemical Kinetics (**)

The saponification (alkaline hydrolysis) of methyl acetate (ethano-ate) can be represented by the following equation:

$$CH_3COOCH_3(aq) + OH^-(aq) \rightarrow CH_3COO^-(aq) + CH_3OH(aq)$$

You are provided with the following reagents:

HA   0·05 M sodium hydroxide.
HB   0·05 M methyl acetate (ethanoate) in water.
HC   0·025 M hydrochloric acid.

All the reactants have been allowed to stand at laboratory conditions for some time until they have attained a constant temperature. Mix HA and HB and allow them to stand for at least 600 s until thermal equilibrium has again been attained. Remove 25 cm³ of the reaction mixture by means of a pipette provided and discharge it into 30 cm³ of cold water in a conical flask, noting the time when the pipette is half empty (start the stop-clock at this stage). *Immediately* titrate the sample with HC using phenolphthalein. Repeat the sampling and titration procedure at 120-s intervals for the first four readings and then carry on at 300-s intervals, stopping after about 2·4 ks.

Tabulate your results under the headings V_t (the volume of acid needed to neutralise the alkali in your sample), $\log_{10}V_t$, $1/V_t$, t. The concentrations of ester and OH^- ion in the sample are equal and are proportional to V_t. Plot graphs of

(a) $\log_{10}V_t$ against t
(b) $1/V_t$ against t

and comment on their form. What is the order of the reaction?

C7   Chemical Kinetics (*)

You are provided with an apparatus suitable for collecting and measuring the volume of gas evolved when a metal reacts with a liquid. It consists, essentially, of a generating vessel (A), a mano-meter (B) containing water, and a syringe (C).

You are required to investigate the volume of hydrogen evolved

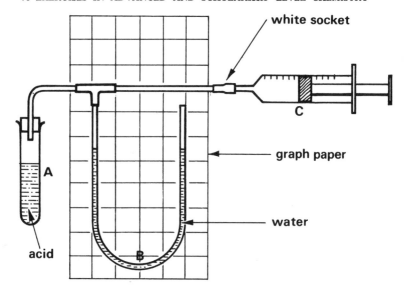

when a given mass of magnesium ribbon is added to dilute hydrochloric acid.

Tie a loose single knot in a piece of cotton about 3 cm from the end. Drop the loop over the piece of magnesium ribbon provided (10 mg) and pull it tight. Into the small test-tube, put about 3 cm depth of the acid (0·5 M hydrochloric) and hold the tube vertically; it is vital that no acid wets the sides of the tube.

Lower the thread and magnesium into the tube, but not too near the surface of the acid, and push the stopper in well—like this:

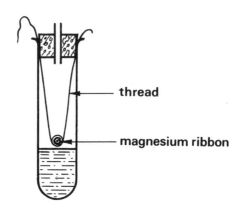

Detach the syringe, push the plunger right in, and attach the nozzle of the syringe to the white socket at the end of the rubber tube.

Ensure that the water level in the manometer is the same in each limb. Holding the syringe in your writing hand, tilt the small test-tube carefully and slowly until the acid just covers the metal. Start your stop-clock *now*. Notice that a gas is evolved and the water in the right-hand limb is pushed down. Pull the plunger of the syringe out slowly to bring the levels in the two arms of the manometer equal again. Keep the levels equal by drawing out the plunger more and more. Record the volume of hydrogen evolved (when the levels of water in the limbs are equal) against time at 1·8 ks intervals until no more gas is evolved. Note that each division marked on the barrel represents 2 cm^3. Try to estimate the volume of gas as accurately as you can.

Plot a graph of volume (cm^3) of hydrogen against time (s). From your graph, deduce the volume of hydrogen that should be evolved by treating 10 mg of magnesium with excess dilute acid. Using the fact that the molar volume of a gas is about 24 dm^3 at room temperature and pressure, state whether your volume estimated is of the correct order of magnitude. Show all working.

From your graph, estimate the initial rate of reaction. Why is this important?

Repeat the experiment using 0·05 M hydrochloric acid in place of 0·1 M. Plot your results in the form of a graph, using the same axes as before. Comment on any differences between this graph and the first one. Deduce the initial rate of reaction and state the ratio of this value to the initial rate in the first part of the experiment. What is the significance of this?

D1   Thermal Chemistry (*)

(*a*) Weigh out between 24·75 and 25·00 g of the salt provided, which is sodium thiosulphate pentahydrate. Show your weighings clearly.

Grind the solid up as finely as possible using the pestle and mortar and transfer all the solid to a clean sheet of paper.

Into the polystyrene cup provided, place 100 cm³ of distilled water and record temperature against time for at least 300 s until the temperature remains steady. At a definite time, rapidly add the powdered salt to the water, stir vigorously, using the thermometer as stirrer, and continue to record the temperature at 30 s intervals until it begins to rise again. The temperature will decrease as the salt dissolves. Plot a graph of temperature against time and, by extrapolation to the time of mixing, obtain as accurately as you can the decrease in temperature at this time.

If m is the weight (in grammes) of salt taken, the weight of solution can be taken as $(100+m)$ g. Take the specific heat capacity of the solution as $4 \cdot 2$ J g^{-1}, calculate the heat of solution in J mol^{-1}. Why was it necessary to powder the salt so finely?

(b) Titrate 25 cm³ (or 20 cm³) portions of standard 1 M potassium permanganate (manganate(VII)) with the solution of sodium thiosulphate from (a), adding excess potassium iodide solution and dilute sulphuric acid to the flask before titrating, so as to liberate iodine. From your results, calculate the molarity of the sodium thiosulphate solution.

$$MnO_4^- + 8H^+ + 5e^- \rightarrow Mn^{2+} + 4H_2O$$

$$2I^- - 2e^- \rightarrow I_2$$

$$I_2 + 2S_2O_3^{2-} \rightarrow 2I^- + S_4O_6^{2-}$$

D2   Thermal Chemistry (*)

(a) Weigh out accurately between 5·75 and 6·00 g of the salt provided, which is sodium chloride. Show your weighings clearly.

Grind the solid up as finely as possible using the pestle and mortar and transfer all the powder to a clean sheet of paper.

Into the polystyrene cup provide, place 100 cm³ of distilled water and record temperature against time for at least 300 s until the temperature remains steady. At a definite time, *rapidly* add the powdered salt to the water, stir vigorously using the thermometer, and continue to record the temperature at 30 s intervals until it begins to rise again. The temperature will decrease as the salt dissolves.

Plot a graph of temperature against time and, by extrapolating to the time of mixing, obtain as accurately as you can the decrease in temperature at this time.

If m is the weight (in grammes) of salt taken, the weight of solution can be taken as $(100+m)$ g. Taking the specific heat capacity of the solution as $4 \cdot 2$ J g^{-1}, calculate the heat of solution in J mol^{-1}. Why was it necessary to powder the salt so finely?

(b) Titrate 25 cm^3 (or 20 cm^3) portions of the salt solution from (a) using standard 1 M silver(I) nitrate solution, HA, with potassium chromate(VI) as indicator. The equation for the reaction is as follows:

$$Ag^+ + Cl^- \rightarrow AgCl \downarrow$$

From your results, calculate the molarity of the chloride ion solution˙

D3 Thermal Chemistry (**)

(a) In the polystyrene cup provided, place 100 cm^3 of distilled water and allow it to stand under room conditions for at least 600 s until the temperature is constant. In the water, suspend 1 g of zinc dust (an excess). Weigh out 1 g of solid iodine and grind this to a fine powder using the pestle and mortar. Rapidly add the iodine to the zinc dust suspended in the water, stir using the thermometer, and record the maximum temperature reached.

In another cup, place 100 cm^3 of distilled water and, after allowing it to attain a constant temperature, dissolve in it 1 g of finely powdered zinc iodide. Again stir and note the maximum temperature reached.

Record all the measurements you have made and, using Hess's Law of Constant Heat Summation, deduce the heat of formation of zinc iodide.

The equations involved in you experiment are:

$$Zn(s) + I_2(s) \rightarrow ZnI_2(aq)$$

$$ZnI_2(s) + aq \rightarrow ZnI_2(aq)$$

(b) In the polystyrene cup provided, place 25 cm^3 of $0 \cdot 2$ M copper(II) sulphate solution and allow to stand for at least 300 s until the temperature is constant.

Weigh out 500 mg (an excess) of iron filings, add rapidly to the contents of the cup, swirl carefully, and record the maximum temperature reached.

From your results, calculate the heat of the reaction

$$Fe(s) + Cu^{2+}(aq) \rightarrow Fe^{2+}(aq) + Cu(s)$$

Comment on the accuracy of your experiments (*a*) and (*b*).

D4   Thermal Chemistry (**)

Solution HA   is standard hydrochloric acid, 1 M.
Solution HB   is sodium hydroxide.
Solution HC   is ammonia solution.

(*a*) Standardise solution HB by titrating 25 cm^3 (or 20 cm^3) portions of HA with HB, using phenolphthalein as indicator. Set out your results clearly in the form of a table.

(*b*) Standardise HC in the same way but using methyl orange as indicator and titrating 25 cm^3 (or 20 cm^3) portions of HC with the acid.

(*c*) Using the measuring cyclinder provided, place 100 cm^3 of HA in the polystyrene cup and allow it to stand for 600 s to attain a steady temperature.

Repeat the procedure using a second cup.

In each case, record the steady temperature (t_1) of the acid. Allow 100 cm^3 of HB and 100 cm^3 of HC to stand in separate beakers until they too have attained steady temperatures (t_2).

In each case, add the alkali rapidly to the acid in the polystyrene cup and stir the mixture with the thermometer (remember to wash it *well* between experiments), recording the maximum temperature reached (t_3).

Take the specific heat capacity of each solution as 4·2 J g^{-1} and calculate the heat changes in the following reactions;

$$HCl(aq) + NaOH(aq) \rightarrow NaCl(aq) + H_2O(l)$$
$$HCl(aq) + NH_3, H_2O(aq) \rightarrow NH_4Cl(aq) + H_2O(l)$$

Comment on any differences in the two results.
Comment on the accuracy of the determinations.

Heat changes should be expressed in joules per mole of salt formed.

Take the temperature rise as $(t_3 - \frac{1}{2}(t_1 + t_2))$.

D5   Thermal Chemistry (**)

You are supplied with:

200 cm^3 of 3 M hydrochloric acid, labelled A.

200 cm^3 of a solution containing 120 g dm^{-3} of a monoacidic base, labelled B.

(a) Prepare 250 cm^3 each of solutions C and D by accurately diluting 25 cm^3 (measured from a burette) of A and B, respectively, with purified water.

Titrate 25 cm^3 portions of D with C, using the indicator provided, and hence calculate the molar weight (relative molecular mass) of the base.

How many cm^3 (=x) of A are equivalent to 25 cm^3 of B?

(b) Carry out this experiment using, as your reaction vessel, a 175 × 30 mm boiling-tube wrapped in cotton wool and inserted into a beaker. Use burettes to measure all volumes and record all temperatures with a thermometer graduated in fifths or tenths of a degree. Take temperature readings as accurately as possible with the aid of a magnifying glass, and *record your results in your notebook*. You may use any watch or clock with a seconds hand with which to measure time. In your calculation, assume that both solutions have unit density and unit thermal capacity.

Into the boiling-tube measure x cm^3 of A. Insert the thermometer and record the temperature at 30 s intervals for 300 s. Then, with continuous stirring, add 25 cm of B and note (i) the time when the addition was begun and (ii) the time when it was complete. Continue to take temperature readings at 30-s intervals, stirring for a few seconds before each reading. Plot a graph of temperature/time for readings before and after addition of B. Extrapolate each portion of the graph to a time corresponding to the addition of 12·5 cm^3 of B, and determine the elevation of temperature at this point. Hence, calculate the heat of neutralisation of the base with hydrochloric acid.

(A.E.B.)

D6 Thermal Chemistry(**)

You are provided with pure borax $(Na_2B_4O_7,10H_2O)$, a solution A of sulphuric acid and a solution B of sodium hydroxide. The molarity of solution B may be taken as twice that of solution A.

You are required to determine:

(a) the molarity of the sulphuric acid solution A by simple titration, and

(b) the heat of neutralisation of sulphuric acid with sodium hydroxide.

Procedure

(i) Prepare a solution containing between 4·70 g and 4·90 g of borax in 250 cm³. The borax should be dissolved initially in warm distilled water and the solution cooled before transfer to a 250 cm³ volumetric flask.

By means of a burette, transfer exactly 25 cm³ of the acid solution A into another 250 cm³ volumetric flask and dilute to the mark. Titrate this *diluted* acid solution against 25 cm³ aliquots of the borax solution, using methyl orange as indicator. The equation in molecular form could be written as

$$Na_2B_4O_7,10H_2O+H_2SO_4 \rightarrow Na_2SO_4+4H_3BO_3+5H_2O$$

(ii) Calculate the molarity of the borax solution and the molarity of the *orginal* acid solution A. Your results should be set out as follows:

Results

Second weighing	.... g
First weighing	.... g
Mass of borax taken	.... g

Titration of the diluted acid solution against 25 cm³ of borax solution
Burette reading (finish)
Burette reading (start)
Volume of solution used

Thus, ... cm³ of diluted acid solution equivalent to 25cm³ of borax solution.

Calculation

(iii) Using the measuring cylinders, transfer *carefully* 50 cm³ of the sulphuric acid solution A into one plastic cup and 50 cm^3 of the sodium hydroxide solution B into the other. Set aside for about 900 s. Place the thermometer provided in the cup containing solution A and record the temperature at 30 s intervals, stirring continuously. At exactly 210 s, pour the entire 50 cm^3 of solution B into the stirred solution A and continue to take temperature readings before from second 240 to second 420.

Your results should be set out as follows:

Results

Time (s) 0·0 30 60 90 120 150 180 210 240 270 300 330 360
Temp (K)
Time (s)   390   420
Temp (K)

Plot a graph of temperature against time on the graph paper provided (temperature on the vertical axis, time on the horizontal axis using a scale of 2 cm to 60 s).

(iv) From the graph, deduce the maximum rise in temperature. Hence calculate the heat of neutralisation of sulphuric acid with sodium hydroxide. It may be assumed that the heat capacity of the final solution is 4·18 J cm^{-3} K^{-1} and that the heat capacities of the thermometer and cup may be neglected.

(L.)

D7   Thermal Chemistry (**)

You are provided with solid sodium chloride, a solution E of silver(I) nitrate and a solution F of barium chloride. The molarity of solution E may be taken as twice that of solution F. You are required to determine:

(*a*) the molarity of the silver nitrate solution E by simple titration, and

(*b*) the heat of reaction of aqueous silver(I) nitrate with aqueous barium chloride.

Procedure

(i) Prepare a solution containing between 1·35 g and 1·55 g of sodium chloride in 250 cm^3. By means of a burette, transfer exactly

50 cm^3 of the silver(I) nitrate solution E into another 254 cm^3 volumetric flask and dilute to the mark. Titrate this diluted silver(I) nitrate solution against 25 cm^3 aliquots of the sodium chloride solution, using potassium chromate as indicator.

(ii) Calculate the molarity of the sodium chloride solution and the molarity of the *original* silver(I) nitrate solution E.

Set out your results as in experiment D6.

(iii) Proceed exactly as in experiment D6 (iii) except that solutions A and B become solutions E and F, respectively.

Set out your results in the same manner.

(iv) From the graph deduce the maximum rise in temperature. Hence calculate the heat of reaction of aqueous silver(I) nitrate with aqueous barium chloride. Make the same assumptions as in experiment D6 section (iv).

(L.)

D8   Thermal Chemistry (**)

The object of this experiment is to measure approximately the heat of neutralisation of sodium phenol-4-sulphonate, which is a weak monobasic acid because of the presence of the phenolic hydroxyl group.

The experiment is carried out by measuring the temperature change on mixing solutions of the sodium phenol-4-sulphonate and sodium hydroxide of known concentrations.

The solutions are mixed in a plastic beaker which has a very low heat capacity and good insulation so that it serves as a simple adiabatic calorimeter; cooling curve corrections are unnecessary, and the small temperature changes involved may be observed directly.

The apparatus is calibrated by mixing hydrochloric acid and sodium hydroxide solutions of known concentrations, and then using the fact that the heat of neutralisation of hydrochloric acid with sodium hydroxide is 58 kJ mol^{-1} under the conditions of the experiment.

The sodium hydroxide solution is standardised against potassium hydrogen phthalate (benzene 1, 2-dicarboxylate), which is a monobasic acid.

HO   is a standard solution of potassium hydrogen phthalate.
HA   is a solution of hydrochloric acid.
HB   is a solution of sodium hydroxide.
HBD   is a solution of HB that has been diluted ten times.
HC   is a solution of sodium phenol-4-sulphonate.

The exact molar concentrations of solutions HO, HA and HC will be given to you by your teacher. A pipette filler must be used because of the corrosive nature of the solutions.

(a) *Standardisation of HB.* The sodium hydroxide solution HB is too concentrated to be used to titrate HO directly and has been diluted tenfold; the diluted solution is HBD.

Take 25 cm^3 portions of solutions HO and titrate with solution HBD using phenolphthalein as indicator.

Calculate the concentration of solution HBD in mol dm^{-3} and hence that of HB.

(b) *Calibration of the apparatus.* Pipette 50 cm^3 of solution HA into one of the plastic beakers and suspend the thermometer in the beaker so that the bulb is immersed but clears the bottom of the beaker. Wait for 120–180 s until a constant temperature is attained, and record the temperature of solution HA.

Remove the beaker and solution from the suspended thermometer and put them on one side. Wipe the thermometer bulb carefully with a tissue, avoiding touching it with the fingers.

Pipette 50 cm^3 of solution HB into another plastic beaker and suspend the thermometer in it. Record the temperature of solution HB.

Into solution HB pour rapidly the 50 cm^3 of solution HA from the first beaker, stirring the mixture carefully with the thermometer. Record the highest temperature attained.

Calculate the temperature change on mixing. If the initial temperatures of solutions HA and HB differ, use the mean.

Repeat the experiment.

(c) *Neutralisation of sodium phenol-4-sulphonate.* Proceed as in (b) but use HC instead of HA.

Repeat the experiment.

(d) *Calculation of the heat of neutralisation of sodium phenol-4-sulphonate.* A correction must first be made for the fact that the solution of acid and base are dilute from 50 cm^3 to 100 cm^3 in experiments (b) and (c). In each case the correction is 1·3 K and must be subtracted from the observed temperature rise to give the net temperature rise.

Assume that the specific heat capacities and densities of all solutions are the same and that the sodium phenol-4-sulphonate reacts completely with sodium hydroxide under the conditions of the experiment.

Calculate:

  (i) the net temperature rise when the acid in 50 cm^3 of HA reacts with the sodium hydroxide in 50 cm^3 of HB;

 (ii) the net temperature rise when the acid in 50 cm^3 of HC reacts with sodium hydroxide in 50 cm^3 of HB;

(iii) the heat of neutralisation of sodium phenol-4-sulphonate under the conditions of this experiment, given that the heat of neutralisation of hydrochloric acid with sodium hydroxide is 58 kJ mol^{-1}.

What do you consider to be an important source of error in your final result?

Set out your results like this:

Concentration of solutions
HO......mol dm^{-3} HA......mol dm^{-3} HC......mol dm^{-3}

(a) *Standardisation of sodium hydroxide*

  Final level
  Initial level
  Titre   Mean titre......... cm^3

  Concentration of sodium hydroxide solutions:
                               HBD........mol dm^{-3}
                               HB........mol dm^{-3}

(b) *Calibration of apparatus*

  Initial temperature of 50 cm^3 of solution
                        HA............   ....
  Initial temperature of 50 cm^3 of solution
                        HB............   ....
  Mean temperature of solutions before mixing
                        ....
  Final temperature after mixing HA/HB
                        ....

Temperature change ....

Mean...........K (x)

(c) *Neutralisation of sodium phenol-4-sulphonate*

Initial temperature of 50 cm^3 of solution HC

....

Initial temperature of 50 cm^3 of solution HB

....

Mean temperature of solutions before mixing

....

Final temperature after mixing HC/HB

....

Temperature change ....

Mean.........K (y)

(d) *Calculation of heat of neutralisation of sodium phenol-4-sulphonate*

$$= \frac{\text{net change of temperature on mixing HC/HB} \times \text{concn HB} \times 58}{\text{net change of temperature on mixing HA/HB} \times \text{concn HC}}$$

$$= \frac{(y-1\cdot3)[\text{HB}]}{(x-1\cdot3)[\text{HC}]} \times 58 = \dots\dots\dots\dots = \dots\dots\dots\dots\text{kJ mol}^{-1}$$

What do you consider to be an important source of error in your final result? ....

(O. and C.)

D9 Thermal Experiment (**)

HA is a fairly concentrated solution of hydrochloric acid.

HB is a fairly concentrated solution of sodium hydroxide.

HC is a standard solution of sodium tetraborate, 0.981 mol dm^{-3}. Sodium tetraborate is a good standard and can be titrated as a base since boric acid (very weak) is liberated.

$$\text{Na}_2\text{B}_4\text{O}_7.10\text{H}_2\text{O} + 2\text{HCl} \rightarrow 2\text{NaCl} + 4\text{H}_3\text{BO}_3 + 5\text{H}_2\text{O}$$

Carefully, using a pipette filler, pipette 20·00 cm^3 of HA into a 200 cm^3 standard flask and make to mark with distilled water. Rinse the pipette with this diluted solution and titrate 20·00 cm^3 portions of it with the HC solution. HC is in the burette. Use bromocresol green as indicator.

Now carry out an *enthalpometric titration* of HB and HA.

Suspend the thermometer so that it is just clear of the bottom of a plastic cup when this is placed underneath. Nearly fill the cup with HA, allow a few minutes for the temperature to stabilise and then read the thermometer. Read to 0·1 degree if possible. By means of a pipette, using a filler, put 50·00 cm^3 of HB in a second beaker and record the temperature. Take the mean of the two temperatures as the initial one.

Carefully suck up 10 cm^3 of HA from the first cup and blow it out into the second (why does this not introduce much error?). Stir with the thermometer and take the temperature when steady. Repeat this procedure until 100 cm^3 of HA have been added. Calculate the rise of temperature from the starting temperature for each reading and multiply the temperature change by a factor, total volume divided by 100. Plot a graph of this quantity against cm^3 of HA added. What can be deduced about the concentration of HB?

Given that the specific heat capacity of the solutions is about 4 kJ kg^{-1}K^{-1}, what is the heat of the reactions between HA and HB?

ORGANIC CHEMISTRY EXERCISES

Observation

Deduction

Simple preparation

General Instructions

Treat the substances provided as described below, and record your observations and inferences. You should attempt to identify any gases evolved. No further experiments should be performed unless told to do so.

It may not always be possible to make a positive identification from the reactions carried out.

In preparing derivatives, it is assumed that students will have available their normal apparatus, preferably semi-micro.

Results

You should have three columns headed

EXPERIMENTS   OBSERVATIONS   INFERENCES

I shall give you just the experiments to carry out, but you should draw out a proper table for each substance in your notebook.

Exercise 1 (*)

Tests (*a*) and (*b*) should be carried out on the solid.

(*a*) Heat a small amount in a hard-glass test tube. Cool and add dilute hydrochloric acid to the residue.

(*b*) Add about 1 cm^3 of concentrated sulphuric acid to a small amount and warm gently.

(*c*) Carry out a flame test on the substance. Tests (*d*) to (*h*) should be carried out on an aqueous solution.

(*d*) Add a few cm^3 of silver(I) nitrate solution and warm the mixture.

(*e*) Add a few cm^3 of mercury(II) chloride solution and warm the mixture.

(*f*) Add a few cm^3 of iron(III) chloride solution and boil.

(*g*) Add ammonium carbonate solution.

(*h*) Add potassium chromate(VI) solution.

Exercise 2 (**)

(*a*) Add 1 cm^3 of concentrated sulphuric acid to an equal bulk of the substance and warm.

(*b*) Treat an aqueous solution with calcium chloride solution (concentrated), then with dilute acetic (ethanoic) adic, then with dilute hydrochloric acid.

(*c*) Acidify an aqueous solution with dilute sulphuric acid; add a few drops of dilute potassium permanganate (manganate(VII)) solution, and warm the mixture.

(*d*) Perform a flame test.

Exercise 3 (*)

(*a*) To a small amount of the solid in a small test-tube, add 1 cm^3 of concentrated sulphuric acid and warm gently.

(*b*) To a small amount of the solid in a small test-tube, add a few cm^3 of dilute sodium hydroxide solution; heat, as there is no reaction in the cold.

(*c*) To a small amount of the solid in a test-tube, add a few cm^3 of dilute sulphuric acid. Bring to the boil and add dilute potassium permanganate (manganate(VII)) solution drop by drop.

(*d*) To a small amount of the solid in a small test-tube, add dilute sodium hydroxide solution. To the resulting suspension add one drop of very dilute copper(II) sulphate solution.

(*e*) Heat a small amount of the solid on a piece of broken porcelain.

Exercise 4 (*)

(*a*) Heat a little of the solid on a piece of broken porcelain, very gently at first, slowly increasing the heat to dull redness.

(*b*) To a small quantity of the solid in a test-tube add a few cm^3 of dilute sulphuric acid and bring to the boil. Pour into an evaporating dish and smell the vapour.

(*c*) To about 1 g of the solid in a test-tube, add about 3 cm^3 of ethanol and, *carefully*, 1 cm^3 of concentrated sulphuric acid. When the heat of mixing has subsided (180 s), warm gently for 300 s, cool, dilute by pouring into an evaporating dish of water, and smell the vapour.

(*d*) To an aqueous solution of the substance in a test-tube add iron(III) chloride solution in the cold; bring to the boil and add dilute hydrochloric acid.

Exercise 5 (*)

(*a*) To a fairly concentrated solution in water, add concentrated nitric acid drop by drop.

(*b*) Heat a little of the solid in a hard-glass test-tube, gently then more strongly. To the *cold* residue, add dilute copper(II) sulphate solution followed by dilute sodium hydroxide solution.

(*c*) To a small amount of the solid, add dilute sodium hydroxide and warm, the boil gently. Test for gases evolved at each stage of the heating.

(*d*) Make a fairly concentrated aqueous solution of the solid and add dilute aqueous sodium nitrite (nitrate(III)) solution; then acidify with dilute hydrochloric acid.

(*e*) Decolourise a few cm^3 of bromine water by adding sodium hydroxide solution, and to this add a portion of a solution of the substance in water.

Exercise 6 (*)

(*a*) Heat a little solid slowly in a test-tube (hard-glass); smell the vapour and try to ignite any gases evolved.

(*b*) Dissolve a small amount of the solid in water and add Fehling's solution; place the tube in a boiling water-bath.

(*c*) Dissolve a small quantity of the solid in water and add ammoniacal silver(I) nitrate solution (add a drop of sodium hydroxide solution to a small volume of silver(I) nitrate solution, then just sufficient dilute ammonia to dissolve the brown precipitate formed). Place the tube in a warm water bath.

(*d*) Treat a solution of the solid in water with 2,4-D.N.P.H. reagent.

(*e*) Treat a little of the solid with a few drops of concentrated sulphuric acid.

Exercise 7 (***)

(a) Heat a little of the solid in a hard-glass test-tube and test any gases or vapours evolved.

(b) In a micro-boiling tube place a little of the solid with an equal bulk of sodium carbonate; moisten with water. Warm and smell carefully. Now heat more strongly and hold flame to mouth of tube.

(c) Add some of the solid to a little dilute sulphuric acid in a micro-boiling tube. Heat and test for any gases and vapours evolved.

(d) Add some of the solid to about 1 cm³ of potassium iodide solution in a test-tube, then add 1 cm³ of sodium hydroxide solution. Add 4 drops of sodium hypochlorite (chlorate(I)) solution and shake. Smell carefully.

(e) Add a small quantity of the solid to a small volume of ammoniacal silver nitrate solution (see Exercise 6). Place the test-tube in a warm water bath and leave for a while.

Exercise 8 (**)

(a) Take 5 drops of the liquid in a small test-tube, boil, and touch a flame to the mouth of the tube while still heating.

(b) In a small test-tube place 2 drops of the liquid, then add 1 drop of dilute sulphuric acid and 2 drops of dilute potassium permanganate (manganate(VII)) solution. Shake and observe. Now heat to boiling.

(c) Into a small test-tube place 1 cm³ of Schiff's reagent, add 1 drop of liquid and shake.

(d) Into a small test-tube place 1 cm³ of 2,4-D.N.P.H. reagent, add 2 drops of liquid and shake.

(e) Into a small test-tube place 1 cm³ of saturated sodium hydrogen sulphite (sulphate(IV)), add 10 drops of the liquid, shake and cool under running water. Set aside and observe.

(f) Into a small test-tube place 2 drops of liquid, 10 drops of potassium iodide solution, 2 drops of sodium hydroxide solution, and shake well. Then add 10 drops of sodium hypochlorite chlorate(I)) solution, shake, stand, and smell.

Exercise 9 (**)

(a) Heat a small amount of the solid on a piece of broken porcelain, gently at first and finally at red heat.

(b) Add a small amount of the solid to about 20 cm³ of bench sodium hydroxide solution in a boiling tube. Shake for a while. Divide the solution into three portions, to be used for (c) to (e).

(c) Add dilute hydrochloric acid in slight excess. Heat slowly to boiling point and then allow to cool.

(d) Add bromine water drop by drop.

(e) Add potassium permanganate (manganate(VII)) solution drop by drop.

(f) Treat a little of the solid with sodium carbonate solution.

Exercise 10 (**)

(a) Heat a small quantity of the solid in a hard-glass test-tube.

(b) To a small quantity of the solid in a hard-glass test-tube, add a few cm³ of sodium hydroxide solution and warm very gently.

(c) Mix a small quantity of the solid with an equal bulk of soda lime and heat the mixture in a hard-glass test-tube, gently at first and then strongly.

(d) To an aqueous solution of the solid, add dilute hydrochloric acid until the solution is acidic to litmus. Then heat to boiling-point, and finally cool.

(e) To an aqueous solution, add iron(III) chloride solution and then dilute hydrochloric acid.

(f) To a small quantity of the solid add a few cm³ of concentrated sulphuric acid and warm gently.

(g) To a small quantity of solid add about 2 cm³ of methanol. Then *cautiously* add a few drops of concentrated sulphuric acid, warm the mixture and pour it into an equal volume of cold water in an evaporating dish. Smell.

Exercise 11 (**)

(a) Place a small quantity of the substance on a piece of broken porcelain and then ignite the substance.

(b) To a small quantity of the solid in a test tube, add a small volume of sodium hydroxide solution and warm gently.

(c) Mix a small amount of the solid with an equal bulk of soda lime and heat the mixture in a hard-glass test tube, gently at first and then strongly.

(*d*) To a solution of the solid in warm water, add iron(III) chloride solution, followed by dilute sulphuric acid.

(*e*) To a solution of the solid in warm water, add bromine water drop by drop.

(*f*) To a little of the solid add sodium carbonate solution.

Exercise 12 (***)

(*a*) Place a small quantity of the solid on a piece of broken porcelain and ignite the substance.

(*b*) To a small quantity of solid in a small test-tube, add an equal bulk of phenol (hydroxybenzene) and a few drops of concentrated sulphuric acid. Heat the mixture, gently at first and then more strongly. Plunge the hot tube into a small volume of water in an evaporating basin, allowing the tube to shatter. Add an excess of sodium hydroxide solution.

(*c*) Mix a small quantity of solid with an equal bulk of soda lime and heat the mixture in a hard-glass test-tube, gently and then more strongly.

(*d*) To a solution of the solid in warm water, add iron(III) chloride solution followed by dilute sulphuric acid.

(*e*) To a solution of the solid in warm water, add bromine water drop by drop.

Exercise 13 (**)

(*a*) Place some of the solid on a piece of broken porcelain and ignite the substance.

(*b*) Prepare a solution of the solid in water and add a few drops of iron(III) chloride solution.

(*c*) Prepare a solution of the substance in water and add sodium hydroxide solution drop by drop until an oil is liberated on the surface. Add bromine water in excess.

(*d*) Treat the substance as in (*c*) to obtain the oil, then shake with a little 'bleaching powder' or sodium hypochlorite (chlorate(I)) solution.

(*e*) Dissolve a small amount of the solid in a small volume of concentrated hydrochloric acid, dilute with a few cm^3 of water and cool under iced water. Add a few drops of a 20% freshly-prepared cold solution of sodium nitrite (nitrate(III)), keeping the original solution still in the ice-bath. Now add the solution formed to a cold solution of 2-naphthol in excess sodium hydroxide solution.

(*f*) Add a few cm³ of chloroform (trichloromethane) to a small amount of solid substance in a small boiling-tube. Then add 2 cm³ of ethanolic sodium hydroxide and warm. Smell.

Exercise 14 (**)

(*a*) Examine the action of heat (gentle and strong) on a small quantity of the solid in a hard-glass test-tube.

(*b*) Warm a little solid with a small volume of concentrated sulphuric acid.

(*c*) Dissolve a little solid in warm dilute hydrochloric acid and then add a small volume of *very* dilute potassium permanganate (manganate(VII)) solution and continue to warm.

(*d*) Dissolve a little of the solid in warm dilute hydrochloric acid, then add an excess of sodium hydroxide solution.

Exercise 15 (***)

(*a*) Heat a small quantity of the solid on a piece of broken porcelain, gently at first and then more strongly.

(*b*) To a small quantity of the solid in a test-tube, add about 1 cm³ of concentrated sulphuric acid and observe any reaction. Then warm gently. Cool, add a little water, followed by excess sodium hydroxide solution.

(*c*) To a fairly concentrated aqueous solution of the solid, add a small volume of fresh iron(III) chloride solution. Do a 'blank' test for comparison in which the substance is omitted and just distilled water is used.

(*d*) To a concentrated solution of the solid add 10% calcium chloride solution in excess. Boil gently. Observe what happens and then add dilute acetic (ethanoic) acid.

Exercise 16   Tosylation (**)

You are provided with a tube, labelled X, and containing an organic compound dissolved in water.

(*a*) To 1 drop of the solution in a small test-tube add 1 drop of iron(III) chloride solution.

(b) To 1 drop of the solution in a small test-tube add 1 drop of Universal Indicator Solution.

(c) To 3 drops of solution in a small test-tube add bromine water dropwise until the reagent is in excess.

(d) To the remaining volume of solution (about 9 cm³), add 10 cm³ of 10% sodium hydroxide solution, followed by a solution of 1g p-toluenesulphonyl chloride (1-methyl-4-chlorosulphonyl benzene) in 3 cm³ acetone (propanone). Swirl the mixture for 600 s, cool under the tap and, if necessary, scratch to induce crystallisation. Filter off the solid at the pump and recrystallise from a little ethanol. Dry a portion of your solid and record the melting-point, which should lie below 373 K. Leave the remainder of your derivative for inspection.

What conclusions can you draw about the nature of X from the tests you have carried out?

Exercise 17 3,5-Dinitrobenzoylation (3,5-Dinitrobenzenecarboxylation) (**)

You are provided with a liquid organic compound in a test-tube, labelled Y.

(a) To about 1 cm³ of the liquid, add a tiny piece of dry sodium. Identify the gas evolved.

(b) Add 2 drops of liquid to a small quantity of phosphorus(V) chloride in a dry test-tube. Carry this out in a fume chamber. Identify the gas evolved.

(c) To 0·5 cm³ of Y add 3 cm³ of 10% potassium solution and 10% sodium hypochlorite (chlorate(I)) solution.

(d) To 500 mg of powdered 3,5-dinitrobenzoyl chloride (3,5-dinitrobenzenecarboxyl chloride) in a dry test-tube, add 2 cm³ of liquid Y and warm the mixture on a water-bath until a clear solution is obtained. Cool and filter off the solid which separates. Recrystallise from light petroleum spirit (b.p. 333 to 353 K) and take the melting point of the pure solid. Leave the remainder of the derivative for inspection. The melting-point should be below 423 K.

What conclusions can you draw about the nature of Y from the experiments you have carried out?

Exercise 18 Formation of a Semicarbazone (***)

You are provided with an organic liquid in a test-tube, labelled Z.

(a) Shake 1 cm^3 of Z with about 0·5 cm^3 of saturated sodium hydrogen sulphite (sulphate(IV)) solution.

(b) Add about 1 cm^3 of Schiff's reagent to 1 cm^3 of Z. Allow the mixture to stand, with shaking from time to time.

(c) Place about 5 cm^3 of silver(I) nitrate solution in a clean test-tube and add 2 drops of dilute sodium hydroxide solution. Add dilute ammonia drop by drop until the precipitated silver(I) oxide has almost redissolved, then add 3 drops of Z. Warm the mixture carefully in a water bath, shaking the tube from time to time to break up any oily lumps present.

(d) Dissolve 3 drops of Z in 2 cm^3 of methanol and then add a few drops of 2,4-D.N.P.H. reagent.

(e) Shake for 180 s approximately 30 drops of Z with 10 cm^3 of ethanol and 50 cm^3 of semicarbazidium chloride ($H_2NOCNHNH_3^+$ Cl$^-$)/sodium acetate (ethanoate) solution. Filter off the precipitate formed and recrystallise it from ethanol. Dry a portion of your product and record its melting-point, which should lie between 443 K and 523 K. Leave the remainder of your derivative for inspection.

What conclusions can you draw about the nature of Z from the experiments you have carried out?

Exercise 20   Acetylation (Ethanoylation) (*)

You are provided with an organic solid P.

(a) Try to dissolve a small quantity of P in dilute hydrochloric acid.

(b) To about 200 mg of P, add a few drops of chloroform (trichloromethane) and then 3 cm^3 of ethanolic sodium hydoxide. Mix well and warm gently. Smell, note the odour, and then cool and add excess concentrated hydrochloric acid to destroy.

(c) Dissolve about 200 mg of P in 1 cm^3 of concentrated hydrochloric acid, dilute by adding 3 cm^3 of water and cool the tube in an ice/water bath. To this add a few drops of freshly prepared cold sodium nitrite (nitrate(III)) solution while keeping the tube under iced water. Add the solution formed to a cold solution of a little 2-naphthol in sodium hydroxide solution.

(d) Place 1 g of P in a small round-bottomed flask, add 5 cm^3 of a mixture containing equal volumes of acetic (ethanoic) acid and acetic (ethanoic) anhydride. Fit the flask with a cold-finger water condenser and reflux the mixture for about 1 ks. Pour the hot mixture into cold water and filter off the solid formed. Recrystallise it from dilute aqueous ethanol and record the melting-point, which should lie between 400 to 450 K. Leave the remainder of your derivative for inspection.

What conclusions can you draw about the nature of P from the experiments you have carried out?

Exercise 20   Investigation (**)

You are provided with a sample of an organic compound X.

(*a*) Dissolve about 100 mg of X in about 10 cm^3 of cold water and add 2–3 drops of phenolphthalein. To this solution add 1 % sodium hydroxide solution drop by drop until the solution is just pink, then a drop or two more until the solution is strongly coloured. Observe the solution.

(*b*) To a similar freshly prepared aqueous solution of X add half its volume of bench ammonia.

(*c*) To another freshly prepared aqueous solution of X add an aqueous solution of phenylhydrazine.

(*d*) Solution Y is a similar solution of X which has been boiled for 3·6 ks. Test it with litmus paper and divide into two. To one of these portions add an aqueous solution of phenylhydrazine and to the other add half its own volume of bench ammonia. Record your observations. Draw what inferences you can about the nature of X and the reactions you have observed.

(Cambridge Open Schol.)

Exercise 21   Investigation (**)

Carry out the following tests on the compound Q provided. From the results draw what conclusions you can about the nature of Q.

(*a*) Test its solubility in water, in aqueous acid, and in aqueous sodium carbonate solutions.

(*b*) Heat in a hard-glass test-tube about 200 mg of Q well mixed, using a mortar, with 1 g of soda lime.

(*c*) Dissolve 200 mg of Q in 4 cm^4 of dilute hydrochloric acid, cool in ice-water, and add 1 cm^3 of the cold 20 % sodium nitrite (nitrate(III)) solution R. Divide the resulting solution into two parts, A and B.

(i) Pour A into a cold alkaline solution of 2-naphthol.

(ii) Boil B for 60 to 120 s, cool, and shake the solution. Then add 1 cm³ of methanol, followed by 1 cm³ of concentrated sulphuric acid (*care*), and heat for 60 s. Pour the solution into cold water in a beaker.

(Cambridge Open Schol.)

Exercise 22   Diazotisation (**)

Test the relative solubility of compound A in dilute hydrochloric acid solution, water, sodium hydrogen carbonate solution and dilute sodium hydroxide solution.

Diazotise a solution of phenylammonium chloride in hydrochloric acid as follows. Dissolve aniline (aminobenzene) (1 cm³) in dilute hydrochloric acid (8 cm³ of 3 M acid) and cool the solution to below 27' K. Add a solution of sodium nitrite (nitrate(III)) in water (2 cm³ of the solution provided, which will contain 800 mg) dropwise, keeping the temperature below 278' K throughout the addition. Pour the resulting solution steadily into a solution of A (the 500 mg provided) in dilute sodium hydroxide (not more than 4 cm³ of 2·5 M reagent), shaking vigorously. An oily precipitate should form. This may crystallise and can be collected directly by suction filtration. If it does not crystallise, decant the aqueous phase, wash the oily drops with water and then add a little ethanol and stir with a glass rod or spatula until the oil has completely crystallised. Collect the crystals by suction filtration and wash them with a little ethanol.

Test the relative solubility of this product in dilute hydrochloric acid, water, sodium hydrogen carbonate solution and dilute sodium hydroxide solution. Leave for inspection, in the filter funnel, the product you do not use in the tests.

Record only your observations on the solubilities of A and your product. Make and record any deductions you can.

(Cambridge Open Schol.)

Exercise 23   Recrystallisation and Mixed Melting-point (**)

You are given a sample of an organic solid, labelled X.

(*a*) To about 1·5 g of this substance, add 20 cm³ of sodium hydroxide solution and boil gently under reflux for 900 s. Identify any gas evolved. Cool the solution, add excess hydrochloric acid, cool and filter off the solid formed. Wash well with cold water and recrystallise a portion from boiling water. Dry and determine the melting-point of your recrystallised sample.

(b) Determine whether your hydrolysis product is identical with the compound Y, which has a relative molecular mass of 122 or 138 (your teacher will tell you which).

(c) Describe the reactions of your hydrolysis product when it is:

(i) heated (dry) with soda lime in a test-tube;

(ii) warmed with a little ethanol and concentrated sulphuric acid.

What can you conclude about the nature of X?

(N.I.)

Exercise 24　Investigation (*)

Carry out the following tests on solid A. Record all your observations and attempt to identify A.

(a) To about 1 cm³ of sodium hydroxide solution add a few crystals of A.

(b) to the product obtained in (a) add an excess of dilute sulphuric acid.

(c) To a few crystals of A add a few drops of iron(III) chloride solution.

(d) Put a few crystals of sodium nitrite (nitrate(III)) in a clean, dry test-tube, add about 500 mg of A and *warm gently* for about 30 s. *Allow to cool* and then add *carefully* twice the volume of concentrated sulphuric acid. Rotate the tube slowly to mix the contents, allowing one or two minutes for any changes to occur.

(e) To about 500 mg of solid A in a clean, dry test-tube add an equal quantity of phthalic anhydride (benzene-1,2-dicarboxylic anhydride), moisten with 2 or 3 drops of concentrated sulphuric acid and *then gently fuse* together for about 60 s. *Allow to cool* to room temperature and then add *most carefully* sodium hydroxide solution, drop by drop, until in excess.

(A.E.B.)

Exercise 25　Acetylation (Ethanoylation) (**)

The substance X is either an aliphatic amine, an aromatic primary amine or a phenol. Its molar weight (relative molecular mass) is 108 to 110.

(a) Classify the compound and determine its melting-point.

(b) To 1 g of the sample in a dry test-tube, add 2·5 cm³ of acetic (ethanoic) anhydride containing 1 drop of concentrated sulphuric acid and shake for about 120 s. If the contents of the tube set solid at this stage, add a little water and stir. Otherwise pour into a little water and stir until the oil solidifies. Filter off the solid and wash it well with cold water. Recrystallise a portion from alcohol/water (2:1), dry, and determine the melting-point.

(c) Suggest possible structural formulae for your acetyl (ethanoyl) derivative, which has a molar weight (relative molecular mass) of about 192–194.

(N.I.)

Exercise 26 (***)

(a) Heat some of the solid in a hard-glass test-tube.

(b) Treat a little of the solid with about 1 cm³ of concentrated sulphuric acid and allow to stand for a while.

(c) Warm a little of the solid with about 1 to 2 cm³ of Fehling's solution in a water-bath.

(d) Repeat (c) but first warm the solid gently for a while with dilute sulphuric acid.

(e) To a small quantity of the solid, add 1 cm³ of distilled water followed by 3 drops of alcoholic 1-naphthol solution. Then pour concentrated sulphuric acid (1 cm³) *carefully* into the reaction mixture to form a separate layer.

(f) Repeat (e) but using concentrated hydrochloric acid (2 to 3 cm³) in place of concentrated sulphuric acid.

(g) Warm a little of the solid with about 1 cm³ of ammoniacal silver nitrate solution (see Exercise 6) in a water bath.

(h) Boil a little of the solid with 1 cm³ of concentrated (30%) sodium hydroxide solution.

Exercise 27 (***)

(a) To a small quantity of the solid in a hard-glass test-tube, add 1 pellet of *dry* sodium. Heat the contents of the tube in a roaring bunsen flame, gently at first and then really strongly. Plunge the red-hot tube into about 10 cm³ of distilled water in an evaporating dish (*care*) and grind up the glass. Filter.

(i) To one portion of the filtrate, add iron(II) sulphate solution, boil and cool. Acidify with dilute sulphuric acid.

(ii) To another portion add sodium pentacyanonitrosylferrate(II) (sodium 'nitroprusside').

(b) Boil a small quantity of bench sodium carbonate solution for a few seconds and cool. Add a small quantity of the solid substance, warm gently, and test for the liberation of carbon dioxide.

(c) To a small quantity of the solid, add 1 cm^3 of chloroform (trichloromethane) and 2 cm^3 of alcoholic sodium hydroxide. Warm and smell. Destroy immediately by putting your tube into a beaker of concentrated hydrochloric acid.

(d) Mix a little of the solid with five times its bulk of soda lime. Grind together and then put the mixture in a hard-glass test-tube. Heat, gently at first and then strongly. Observe the odour. Remove a few drops of the liquid which forms on the sides of the tube and treat with sodium hypochlorite (sodium chlorate(I)) solution.

(e) (i) Dissolve a small quantity of the solid in 2 cm^3 of 10% sodium carbonate solution, cool in an ice/water bath and add a pre-cooled fresh solution of sodium nitrite (nitrate(III)). Add 1 cm^3 of dilute hydrochloric acid and keep in an ice/water-bath.

(ii) Dissolve two drops of dimethylaniline (dimethylaminobenzene) in 1 cm^3 of dilute hydrochloric acid, cool in an ice/water bath, and add slowly to (i). Make alkaline with sodium hydroxide solution.

Exercise 28 (***)

(a) In an ordinary test-tube, add enough solid to cover the bottom, then 2 cm^3 of sodium hydroxide solution, and warm gently. Two layers are formed:

$$A = \text{upper layer} \qquad B = \text{lower layer.}$$

Extract a drop of B by means of a micropipette, place in a small test-tube, add 2 drops of ethanol and 1 pellet of potassium hydroxide, then 1 drop of aniline (aminobenzene). Warm and smell. Sink the tube in a beaker of concentrated hydrochloric acid *immediately* you have finished this part of the experiment.

(b) To a few drops of A add a few drops of dilute acetic (ethanoic) acid and 1 drop of mercury(II) chloride solution. Warm.

(c) In a micro-boiling tube place about 1 micro-spatula full of powdered solid and then add 5 drops of concentrated sulphuric acid, shake and stand. Observe and smell.

(*d*) To a small quantity of the solid add 2 cm³ of Fehling's solution in a micro-boiling tube. Heat gently. Smell.

(*e*) To a small volume of silver(I) nitrate solution in a micro-boiling tube, add 1 drop of sodium hydroxide solution and just enough ammonia to dissolve the precipitate formed (of what?). Add a small quantity of the solid and warm. Observe.

(*f*) To a small quantity of powdered solid in a micro-boiling tube, add 2 cm³ of saturated sodium hydrogen sulphite (sulphate(IV)) and cool under running water from the cold tap. Observe what happens.

Exercise 29   Investigation (**)

You are provided with two organic liquids X and Y, each having C, H, O only. Test each as follows:

(*a*) Add an equal amount of cold water to the liquid. Warm, then cool, then add sodium carbonate (as the solid).

(*b*) To the liquid in a *dry* beaker, add a small quantity of phosphorus (V) chloride (with great care); do this in the fume chamber.

(*c*) Mix equal volumes of X and Y, heat (not boil) and pour the mixture into dilute sodium carbonate solution.

What do you conclude from your observations so far?

Carry out *two* further experiments which test your inferences (any inference you have made can be tested).

For all your experiments make comments on the scale you use and on the chemical changes involved.

Write up your results in the form of a table.

Exercise 30   Investigation (**)

You are given three organic compounds, X, Y and Z. Each contains C, H and O only. They are liquids and are *inflammable*.

Carry out the following tests on each.

(*a*) Observe its odour.

(*b*) Pour a drop or two into some 2,4-D.N.P.H. reagent (i.e. 2,4-dinitrophenylhydrazine), mix well, and stand for a while.

(*c*) Pour 1 cm³ into a clean dry crucible and ignite the liquid.

(*d*) To about 2 cm³ of the liquid in a dry test-tube add (with care) 1 pellet of sodium hydroxide and shake.

Make what inferences you can about the natures of X, Y and Z.

Carry out three further experiments that test any of the inferences you have made.

Quote the scale of your experiments and write up your results in tabular form.

Exercise 31   Investigation (*)

The substance HX is a neutral methyl ester of an organic acid. Treat HX as described below and record your obcervations and inferences.

Note: For experiments (*b*) and (*c*), a suitable quantity of HX is about 300 to 400 mg—about enough to cover a new penny piece generously. A much smaller quantity of HX will suffice for (*a*). You are reminded that 880 ammonia is best handled in the fume cupboard.

(*a*) Dissolve a small quantity of HX in water and test the solution with litmus paper.

(*b*) Make a solution of HX in a few cm³ of water and, after about 200 s have elapsed, add a few drops of calcium chloride solution. Having observed the effect of calcium chloride solution, make the mixture strongly acidic with dilute hydrochloric acid.

(*c*) In a test tube, dissolve a quantity of HX in a few cm³ of water by shaking the tube vigorously. *Immediately* add 1–2 cm³ of 880 ammonia. Shake thoroughly and allow the mixture to stand for about 200 s. Filter off the solid product at the pump and wash it thoroughly with cold water until it no longer smells of ammonia. Carry out the following tests on this moist, solid product, HY.

(i) Shake a sample of HY with cold, dilute sodium hydroxide solution. Having observed the effect (if any) of cold sodium hydroxide, boil the mixture thoroughly.

(ii) Shake a sample of HY with cold dilute sodium hydroxide solution, and then add a few drops of dilute copper(II) sulphate solution.

Summarise your conclusions about the natures of HX and HY and the conversion of HX to HY.

(O. and C.)

INORGANIC CHEMISTRY EXERCISES

Observation

Deduction

Simple Preparation

General Instructions

Carry out the observation/deduction exercises as indicated. You may use any textbook you like when carrying out further experiments to test your inferences.

Full credit cannot be given unless you record accurately your observations, deductions and method (including scale of experiments).

Results should be presented in tabular form.

Unless otherwise stated, your experiment(s) to test your inferences can relate to the cation or anion.

Results

You should have three columns headed

EXPERIMENTS   METHOD/OBSERVATIONS   INFERENCES

I shall give you just the experiments to carry out, but you should draw out a proper table for each substance in your notebook.

Exercise 1 (*)

You are provided with two simple salts, X and Y. Make an aqueous solution of each one and then carry out the tests shown below on each solution separately.

For each salt, given one further experiment to test your inferences about the nature of the cation in X and in Y.

(a) To the solution, add dilute hydrochloric acid followed by barium chloride solution.

(b) To the solution, add sodium hydroxide solution, a small volume first and then an excess.

(c) To the solution, add bench dilute ammonia solution, a small volume at first and then an excess.

Exercise 2 (**)

You are provided with two simple salts, X and Y. Carry out the tests shown below on each of the salts and state what tentative inferences you draw. For each salt, carry out two further experiments which satisfactorily test any of your inferences.

(*a*) Perform a flame test on the solid.

(*b*) Mix a little of the salt with a small quantity of potassium dichromate(VI) and then warm with concentrated sulphuric acid.

Exercise 3 (*)

You are provided with two simple salts, X and Y. Carry out the tests shown below on each salt and state what tentative inferences you draw. Use a fairly concentrated aqueous solution of each salt. For each salt carry out one further experiment to test any of your inferences.

(*a*) To the solution, add potassium iodide solution.

(*b*) To the solution, add tin(II) chloride solution and allow to stand.

(*c*) To the solution, add ammonium sulphide (or hydrogen sulphide) solution.

(*d*) To the solution, add dilute nitric acid and silver(I) nitrate solution.

(*e*) To the solution, add iron(II) sulphate solution in equal volume, filter (if necessary) and then pour concentrated sulphuric acid into the tube, held at an angle to the vertical.

Exercise 4 (**)

You are provided with two simple salts, X and Y. Carry out the tests shown below on each salt and state what tentative inferences you can draw. Use fairly concentrated aqueous solutions of each salt.

For each salt, carry out two further experiments which satisfactorily test any of your inferences.

(*a*) To the solution, add dilute nitric acid and silver(I) nitrate solution.

(*b*) To the solution, add concentrated ammonium carbonate solution.

(*c*) To the solution, add potassium chromate(VI) solution.

(*d*) To a very dilute solution, add dilute sulphuric acid.

Exercise 5 (*)

You are provided with three sodium salts, X, Y and Z. Carry out the tests shown below for each salt and state what tentative inferences you can draw.

For each salt, carry out one further experiment which satisfactorily tests any of your inferences.

(*a*) Examine the action of heat on the solid in a small hard-glass test-tube.

(*b*) Treat the solid with dilute hydrochloric acid in the cold and identify any gases evolved. For Y only, examine the effect of adding dilute hydrochloric acid to an aqueous solution of the salt.

(*c*) To an aqueous solution of the salt, add magnesium sulphate solution.

(*d*) Add an aqueous solution of the salt to a dilute solution of potassium permanganate (manganate(VII)).

Exercise 6 (*)

You are provided with two solutions, X and Y. Carry out the tests on them as indicated below. From your results of these experiments only, what conclusions can you draw concerning the nature of X and of Y?

(*a*) Add a little of solution X to a dilute solution of potassium iodide, acidified with dilute sulphuric acid.

(*b*) Add a little of solution X to a *very* dilute solution of potassium permanganate (manganate(VII)) acidified with dilute sulphuric acid.

(*c*) Add a little of solution X to potassium dichromate(VI) solution acidified with dilute sulphuric acid; add ether (ethoxyethane) and shake.

(*d*) Add a little of solution X to a small amount of lead(II) sulphide in a test tube.

(*e*) Add a little of solution X to iron(II) sulphate solution acidified with dilute sulphuric acid.

(*f*) Add a little of solution Y to a dilute solution of potassium permanganate (manganate(VII)) acidified with dilute sulphuric acid.

(*g*) Add a little of solution Y to a dilute solution of potassium dichromate(VI) acidified with dilute sulphuric acid.

(*h*) To a little of solution Y, add barium chloride solution.

(*i*) Repeat test (*h*) on solution Y but *first* add dilute hydrochloric acid.

Exercise 7 (*)

The red powder provided is mercury(II) oxide, which does not dissolve in water, and substance X is a simple salt.

Carry out the tests below and state what tentative inferences you draw. Carry out and describe two further experiments which satisfactorily test any of these inferences.

(*a*) Test a solution of X in water with litmus paper.

(*b*) Add an excess of the solution of X in water to a little mercury(II) oxide and again test the solution with litmus paper.

(*c*) Boil a solution of mercury(II) oxide in X solution with a solution of potassium dichromate(VI), acidified with dilute sulphuric acid.

(*d*) Treat the products from reaction (*c*) with excess sodium thiosulphate crystals.

Exercise 8 (**)

You are provided with two substances, X and Y. Each is a simple salt. Dissolve X and Y separately in distilled water. Describe as fully as you can what happens when solutions of X and Y are separately treated as shown below. What tentative inferences can you draw?

(*a*) Solution treated with litmus.

(*b*) Solution treated with a solution of potassium chromate(VI). Mix the two solutions of X and Y. What further inferences can now be drawn?

On each substance, now carry out one more experiment that satisfactorily tests any of your inferences.

Exercise 9 (**)

You are provided with two substances, X and Y. X is a simple salt and Y is a mixture of two simple salts. Describe as carefully and as fully as you can what happens when each substance is treated as shown below. State what tentative inferences you can draw and then carry out two further experiments that satisfactorily test your inferences.

(*a*) Treat the substance with cold concentrated sulphuric acid.

(*b*) Treat the substance with concentrated sulphuric acid and then warm carefully and gently.

(*c*) Treat an aqueous solution of the substance with silver(I) nitrate solution.

Exercise 10 (*)

You are provided with a solution of a substance X. Describe as fully as you can what happens when the following experiments are performed. What conclusions can you make about the nature of the anion in X?

(*a*) Add dilute hydrochloric acid to a few cm^3 of X solution, and identify the gas evolved.

(*b*) Add a small volume of X solution to a few cm^3 of dilute potassium iodide solution; then add a little starch solution.

(*c*) Add a small volume of X solution to a few cm^3 of lead(II) nitrate solution and then boil.

(*d*) Add a few drops of cobalt(II) nitrate solution to a few cm^3 of X solution. Notice what happens, then warm gently and identify any gas which is evolved.

Exercise 11   Investigation/Preparation (***)

You are provided with two samples, A and B, of a simple substance containing two radicals.

(*a*) Use A to identify the two radicals.

(*b*) Use the whole of B in the following preparation.

Dissolve B in about 20 cm^3 of water and slowly add the solution to about 25 cm^3 of dilute potassium hydroxide solution in a conical flask, swirling the flask frequently. Add 50 cm^3 of the hydrogen peroxide solution provided; add a few boiling chips and boil the solution gently until it turns yellow; continue boiling until the volume of solution is about 30 cm^3. *Allow the solution to cool* and add glacial acetic (ethanoic) acid drop by drop until there is a colour change; add a further 1 cm^3. Boil until the volume of solution is about 25 cm^3 and then cool the solution in ice. Filter the product under suction and wash it with two 5 cm^3 portions of ethanol.

Dry and weigh the crystals. Record your yield and leave your product clearly labelled for inspection.

How do you interpret the reactions?

(Cambridge Open Schol.)

Exercise 12 (**)

You are provided with a solid salt X and you are required to carry out the experiments shown in the following sequence on it. For (*a*) and (*b*) use the solid and for the remainder use a dilute aqueous solution. What conclusions do you have about the nature of the anion in X?

(*a*) Heat gently a small amount of X with concentrated hydrochloric acid. Identify any gases evolved.

(*b*) Mix a small quantity of sodium chloride with about three times its weight of X. Add an equal volume of concentrated sulphuric acid and warm.

(*c*) To the solution, add barium chloride solution, followed by dilute hydrochloric acid.

(*d*) To the solution, add dilute sulphuric acid, then having observed what happens add sodium hydroxide solution until it is in excess.

(*e*) To the solution, add silver(I) nitrate solution, followed by dilute nitric acid.

(*f*) To the solution, add lead(II) nitrate solution, followed by dilute nitric acid.

(*g*) To a small volume of solution, add dilute sulphuric acid and dilute hydrogen peroxide solution.

(*h*) To the solution, add dilute sulphuric acid and dilute sodium sulphite (sulphate(IV)) solution.

Exercise 13   Redox (*)

You are provided with five solutions, P, Q, R, S and T. P is a solution of potassium iodide. Using small volumes (drops on a white tile or in small test-tubes) of these solutions, investigate the following combinations (*adding reagents to each other in the order stated*).

$$P+Q$$
$$P+Q+R$$

$$P + Q + S$$
$$Q + R + S$$
$$P + Q + R + S$$

Record all that you observe and deduce what you can about Q, R and S.

Using the five solutions only, find out whether solution T contains an oxidising agent, a reducing agent or neither. Record all your observations and deductions.

(O. and C.)

Exercise 14   Combined Investigatory/Titrimetry Exercise (***)

(a) Weigh out accurately between 9·5 and 10·5 grammes of the salt HX, dissolve it in water, and make the solution to 250 cm^3 (or 200 cm^3) in a graduated flask.

Record your weighings and the volume of the flask.

Titrate 25 cm^3 (or 20 cm^3) portions of HX solution as follows.

Add to each portion an excess of solid potassium iodide and titrate the liberated iodine with the standard solution of sodium thiosulphate, HY, which contains 25.00 g dm^{-3} of $Na_2S_2O_3.5H_2O$ crystals. Use starch solution as indicator. A light-coloured precipitate will be present in the titration flask throughout the titration, and the end-point is when the last traces of the dark blue starch/iodine colour have disappeared and the only thing to remain in the flask is the precipitate, suspended in a colourless liquid.

Record the volume of your pipette and all burette readings.

From your results, calculate the number of moles of HX per cubic decimetre of solution.

(b) Carry out the following tests on HX and record all your observations.

(i) Add aqueous ammonia to a small volume of your solution until the ammonia is present in excess.

(ii) To a little solid HX, add about 2–3 cm^3 of bench dilute sodium hydroxide solution and heat the mixture. Identify any gas evolved.

(iii) To a small volume of your solution of HX, add dilute hydrochloric acid followed by barium chloride (or nitrate) solution.

(iv) Perform a flame test on the solid HX.

Discuss briefly what conclusions you can draw from your observations, and say what you think is the nature of HX.

Exercise 15   Inorganic chase (**)

You are provided with unlabelled (but numbered) tubes containing the following (list I) white solids, together with some sticky labels. The idea of this exercise is to label each tube correctly. You have access *only* to the substances shown in list II.

List I

Sodium iodide, potassium chloride, sodium hydrogen carbonate, lead carbonate, magnesium sulphate, ammonium chloride, sodium orthophosphate (phosphate(V)), zinc sulphate, aluminium sulphate, calcium carbonate, barium nitrate, zinc sulphide.

List II

Laboratory mineral acids, silver nitrate solution, hydrogen sulphide solution, sodium hydroxide solution, distilled water, litmus solution, flame testing equipment, potassium chromate(VI) solution, dilute ammonia solution, barium chloride solution.

You may use test-tubes for carrying out reactions.

Describe carefully your method of approach to this problem and label the tubes correctly, leaving them for inspection.

Exercise 16   Investigation (***)

Examine the effect of heat on each of the substances, P, Q and R. Make solutions of P, Q and R separately in dilute nitric acid.

Examine the reactions of these solutions with (*a*) sodium hydroxide solution, (*b*) concentrated hydrochloric acid, (*c*) sodium hypochlorite (chlorate(I)) solution.

Describe what you observe and draw what conclusions you can as to the identity of P, Q and R. Explain where possible the reactions observed.

(O. and C.)

Exercise 17   Investigation (***)

S, T and U are three metallic oxides.

(*a*) Examine the solubility of these oxides in water. Note whether the solution is acidic, neutral or alkaline. Examine also the solubilities of the oxides in dilute and concentrated hydrochloric acid, and in sodium hydroxide solution. (Use very little of the solids for this purpose.)

(*b*) To small portions of each oxide, add some water and an equal quantity of concentrated hydrochloric acid. Then add a little zinc filings or granulated zinc. Warm, if necessary. Record your observations.

(*c*) Repeat experiment (*b*) using potassium iodide solution in place of the zinc.

Draw any conclusions you can about the nature of the oxides. You are not asked to identify them.

(O. and C.)

Exercise 18   Investigation (**)

Carry out the following experiments on substance X:

(*a*) Heat it.

(*b*) Heat it with solid sodium acetate (ethanoate).

(*c*) To its solution in dilute sulphuric acid, add a few drops of potassium permanganate (manganate(VII)) solution and warm.

(*d*) To its solution in water, add silver(I) nitrate solution.

(*e*) To its solution in water, add ammonia solution gradually until no further action is seen. To the resulting solution add a few drops of silver(I) nitrate solution and warm gently.

Say what you think X is and give what explanations you can of the reactions you have observed.

Exercise 19   Investigation (**)

Carry out the following experiments on substance A:

(*a*) Examine its solubility in water.

(*b*) To a small portion of A, add dilute nitric acid and warm it until there is no further action taking place.

(*c*) To separate volumes of the solution from (*b*),

(i) add sodium hydroxide solution and warm,

(ii) add bench dilute ammonia solution.

(*d*) Dissolve a small quantity of A in sodium thiosulphate solution. Take separate volumes of this solution and

(i) add sodium hydroxide solution and warm,

(ii) add dilute sulphuric acid and warm.

Record all your observations and say what you think A could be. Suggest explanations for the reactions you have observed.

Exercise 20 Investigation (***)

Carry out the following experiments on substance P:

(a) Dissolve a portion of it in concentrated hydrochloric acid. Dilute the solution, redissolving any precipitate in the minimum amount of hydrochloric acid. Call this solution S.

(b) To a portion of S, add ammonia solution at first gradually and then in excess.

(c) To another portion of S, add sodium hydroxide solution at first gradually and then in excess.

(d) To another portion of S, add hydrogen sulphide solution. If any precipitate forms here, try to dissolve it in (i) yellow ammonium polysulphide, (ii) dilute nitric acid.

(e) To a portion of S, add a solution obtained by dissolving a few crystals of potassium iodide in dilute hydrochloric acid. Add the reagent gradually at first, then in excess.

(f) To a portion of S, add sodium thiosulphate solution and warm.

Describe and account for what you observe in each experiment and try to indicate the nature of P. You are not required to identify it.

Exercise 21 The Electrochemical Series (*)

You are provided with a supply of dilute sulphuric acid and powdered samples of four different metals, labelled V, W, X and Y.

Investigate the relative speeds with which these metals liberate hydrogen from the acid, judging this by (a) rate of evolution of hydrogen bubbles, (b) rate of solution of the metal in the acid.

You will have to devise and use standard conditions (volume of acid, temperature, etc.) for these tests. Record briefly what these conditions are and what results you obtain. From these results, put the four metals in order of reactivity.

(O. and C.)

Exercise 22 Combined Investigation/Titrimetry Exercise (**)

(a) Weigh out accurately between 600 mg and 800 mg of the salt CI provided, dissolve it in water, and make up the solution with water to 250 cm^3 or 200 cm^3 in a graduated flask.

Record your weighings and the volume of your graduated flask. Titrate 25·0 cm^3 or 20·0 cm^3 portions of this solution as follows.

To each, add an excess of potassium iodide, followed by 5 cm³ of 4M hydrochloric acid and two drops of catalyst solution provided. Titrate the liberated iodine *without delay* with the sodium thiosulphate solution provide, which contains 25·00 g $Na_2S_2O_3.5H_2O$ per 1,000 cm³.

Record the volume of your pipette and all burette readings.

Calculate the number of moles of CI per 1 000 cm³ of your solution.

(*b*) Carry out the following tests on CI and report your observations:

(i) Heat a little solid CI in a dry Pyrex test-tube until decomposition begins; continue heating so that decomposition proceeds for about 15 s. Leave the tube to cool to room temperature.

(ii) Add water to the residue in the cold tube. Test the resulting solution with aqueous silver(I) nitrate solution, followed by dilute ammonia.

(iii) Dissolve a little CI in water in a test tube, and add aqueous silver(I) nitrate followed by dilute ammonia.

(iv) Add 3 M sulphuric acid and a little oxalic (ethanedioic) acid to an excess of fairly concentrated aqueous CI solution in a test-tube. Boil the mixture.

Discuss briefly what conclusions can be drawn from your observations, and state what you can about the nature of CI.

(N.I.)

Exercise 23 Preparation/Investigation (***)

You are provided with a quantity of an oxide of a metal M and, in the first part of this exercise you are required to convert it to the sulphate of M.

You are provided with a solution of oxalic (ethanedioic) acid in dilute sulphuric acid.

Add the oxide to the oxalic (ethanedioic) acid solution in sulphuric acid in the beaker provided and cover the beaker with a watch-glass to prevent the loss of material by spray. When the reaction has subsided, filter (using an ordinary filter apparatus) and evaporate the filtrate to concentrate it (evaporate to at least one-third bulk). Allow the solution to cool and filter off the crystals formed using a Büchner apparatus. Wash the crystals with ethanol, then ether (ethoxyethane) and then allow them to dry in air. Allow your crystals to stand for inspection on a clean sheet of filter paper and use as small a portion as possible for the following experiments.

(a) To an aqueous solution of the sulphate, add sodium hydroxide solution until this is in excess; allow the precipitate formed to stand in the air while you perform the remainder of the experiments.

(b) To an aqueous solution of the sulphate, add dilute ammonia solution, followed by ammonium chloride solution. Shake.

(c) To an aqueous solution of the sulphate, add hydrogen sulphide solution.

(d) Boil a dilute solution of the sulphate with a little solid lead(VI) oxide and a little concentrated nitric acid. Dilute considerably and allow to settle.

What can you infer about the nature of M? In the preparation, why was oxalic (ethanedioic) acid used? What was the oxide used in the preparation?

Exercise 24   Preparation/Investigation (***)

You are provided with a solution of ammonium chloride in water and a sample of a hydrated chloride. Bring the ammonium chloride solution to the boil in the boiling-tube and then stir in the chloride. Into a beaker, place decolorising charcoal and then add the hot reaction mixture, stir, and cool the beaker under running water from the cold tap. Add concentrated ammonia solution (40 cm^3) to the contents of the beaker (do this in the fume chamber) and then cool this in an ice/water bath. Add slowly, in portions, 35 cm^3 of 20-volume hydrogen peroxide solution, shaking vigorously after each addition. Heat the mixture in a water bath at 333 K for about 200 s and maintain it at this temperature until the pink colour has completely gone; stir and shake constantly. Cool again in the ice/water bath and notice that crystals are formed. Filter these off using a Buchner apparatus and transfer the crude solid to a beaker containing 150 cm^3 of boiling water and 5 cm^3 of concentrated hydrochloric acid. Filter hot and, to the filtrate, add 20 cm^3 of concentrated hydrochloric acid and cool in the ice/water bath. Filter off the crystals formed using the Buchner apparatus and leave the crystals on a dry piece of filter paper for inspection.

(b) Perform the following tests on an aqueous solution of the hydrated chloride, which was used in (a).

(i) Add sodium hydroxide solution, then ammonium chloride solution, and shake.

(ii) Add dilute ammonia solution until this is present in excess.

(iii) Add hydrogen sulphide solution.

(iv) To a *concentrated* solution, acidified with acetic (ethanoic) acid, add an excess of a concentrated solution of potassium nitrite (nitrate(III)).

(v) Add a few crystals of ammonium thiocyanate to the solution, followed by pentanol (amyl alcohol). Shake and examine the alcohol layer.

What do you conclude about the nature of the cation in the hydrated chloride?

Write down the probable formula of the complex salt you have prepared in part (*a*) of this exercise.

INORGANIC CHEMISTRY EXERCISES

Simple salts

General Instructions

In recent years, examination boards have been setting, for the most part, a simple salt to be identified as part of the A/S level practical chemistry examination. It is advisable that students should have regular practice at this, taken over the two-year course. In fact many teachers will begin their instruction in analysis at O-level.

It is suggested that teachers draw up a list of possible cations and anions to be identified and confirmed, based on the requirements of their own G.C.E. Board, and then select suitable salts for the students to practise on, say, once per week. A convenient way of allocating salts to students is as follows, based on an idea of Dr. R. D. Gidden.

For each student in the class the teacher in charge has a grid of possible cations and anions to be identified, as shown. As the students identify correctly a given salt they have this salt ticked off on the grid. The numbers allocated to salts are completely random, so there is no way of a student knowing in advance what to expect. The grid can be divided up (as far as cations is concerned) into the normal qualitative groups, so that the teacher can see at a glance which areas of the analysis the student should practise.

The student should be encouraged to set out his/her analysis under the headings EXPERIMENT, METHOD AND OBSERVATIONS, INFERENCES, and to include both preliminary tests as well as systematic analysis. Their tables should be divided into CATION ANALYSIS and ANION ANALYSIS. For each ion inferred, they should be encouraged to give one or two confirmatory tests.

It is suggested that a definite range of analysis is used during the first phase of the course and the remainder during the second phase. A typical sequence is shown in the Supervisors' booklet, but others can be added if the teacher requires. Analysis of a few commercial materials provides an interesting diversion.

Logarithmic Tables

LOGARITHMS

	0	1	2	3	4	5	6	7	8	9	1	2	3	4	5	6	7	8	9
10	·0000	0043	0086	0128	0170	0212	0253	0294	0334	0374	4	8	12	17	21	25	29	33	37
11	·0414	0453	0492	0531	0569	0607	0645	0682	0719	0755	4	8	11	15	19	23	26	30	34
12	·0792	0828	0864	0899	0934	0969	1004	1038	1072	1106	3	7	10	14	17	21	24	28	31
13	·1139	1173	1206	1239	1271	1303	1335	1367	1399	1430	3	6	10	13	16	19	23	26	29
14	·1461	1492	1523	1553	1584	1614	1644	1673	1703	1732	3	6	9	12	15	18	21	24	27
15	·1761	1790	1818	1847	1875	1903	1931	1959	1987	2014	3	6	8	11	14	17	20	22	25
16	·2041	2068	2095	2122	2148	2175	2201	2227	2253	2279	3	5	8	11	13	16	18	21	24
17	·2304	2330	2355	2380	2405	2430	2455	2480	2504	2529	2	5	7	10	12	15	17	20	22
18	·2553	2577	2601	2625	2648	2672	2695	2718	2742	2765	2	5	7	9	12	14	16	19	21
19	·2788	2810	2833	2856	2878	2900	2923	2945	2967	2989	2	4	7	9	11	13	16	18	20
20	·3010	3032	3054	3075	3096	3118	3139	3160	3181	3201	2	4	6	8	11	13	15	17	19
21	·3222	3243	3263	3284	3304	3324	3345	3365	3385	3404	2	4	6	8	10	12	14	16	18
22	·3424	3444	3464	3483	3502	3522	3541	3560	3579	3598	2	4	6	8	10	12	14	15	17
23	·3617	3636	3655	3674	3692	3711	3729	3747	3766	3784	2	4	6	7	9	11	13	15	17
24	·3802	3820	3838	3856	3874	3892	3909	3927	3945	3962	2	4	5	7	9	11	12	14	16
25	·3979	3997	4014	4031	4048	4065	4082	4099	4116	4133	2	3	5	7	9	10	12	14	15
26	·4150	4166	4183	4200	4216	4232	4249	4265	4281	4298	2	3	5	7	8	10	11	13	15
27	·4314	4330	4346	4362	4378	4393	4409	4425	4440	4456	2	3	5	6	8	9	11	13	14
28	·4472	4487	4502	4518	4533	4548	4564	4579	4594	4609	2	3	5	6	8	9	11	12	14
29	·4624	4639	4654	4669	4683	4698	4713	4728	4742	4757	1	3	4	6	7	9	10	12	13
30	·4771	4786	4800	4814	4829	4843	4857	4871	4886	4900	1	3	4	6	7	9	10	11	13
31	·4914	4928	4942	4955	4969	4983	4997	5011	5024	5038	1	3	4	6	7	8	10	11	12
32	·5051	5065	5079	5092	5105	5119	5132	5145	5159	5172	1	3	4	5	7	8	9	11	12
33	·5185	5198	5211	5224	5237	5250	5263	5276	5289	5302	1	3	4	5	6	8	9	10	12
34	·5315	5328	5340	5353	5366	5378	5391	5403	5416	5428	1	3	4	5	6	8	9	10	11
35	·5441	5453	5465	5478	5490	5502	5514	5527	5539	5551	1	2	4	5	6	7	9	10	11
36	·5563	5575	5587	5599	5611	5623	5635	5647	5658	5670	1	2	4	5	6	7	8	10	11
37	·5682	5694	5705	5717	5729	5740	5752	5763	5775	5786	1	2	3	5	6	7	8	9	10
38	·5798	5809	5821	5832	5843	5855	5866	5877	5888	5899	1	2	3	5	6	7	8	9	10
39	·5911	5922	5933	5944	5955	5966	5977	5988	5999	6010	1	2	3	4	5	7	8	9	10
40	·6021	6031	6042	6053	6064	6075	6085	6096	6107	6117	1	2	3	4	5	6	8	9	10
41	·6128	6138	6149	6160	6170	6180	6191	6201	6212	6222	1	2	3	4	5	6	7	8	9
42	·6232	6243	6253	6263	6274	6284	6294	6304	6314	6325	1	2	3	4	5	6	7	8	9
43	·6335	6345	6355	6365	6375	6385	6395	6405	6415	6425	1	2	3	4	5	6	7	8	9
44	·6435	6444	6454	6464	6474	6484	6493	6503	6513	6522	1	2	3	4	5	6	7	8	9
45	·6532	6542	6551	6561	6571	6580	6590	6599	6609	6618	1	2	3	4	5	6	7	8	9
46	·6628	6637	6646	6656	6665	6675	6684	6693	6702	6712	1	2	3	4	5	6	7	7	8
47	·6721	6730	6739	6749	6758	6767	6776	6785	6794	6803	1	2	3	4	5	5	6	7	8
48	·6812	6821	6830	6839	6848	6857	6866	6875	6884	6893	1	2	3	4	4	5	6	7	8
49	·6902	6911	6920	6928	6937	6946	6955	6964	6972	6981	1	2	3	4	4	5	6	7	8
50	·6990	6998	7007	7016	7024	7033	7042	7050	7059	7067	1	2	3	3	4	5	6	7	8
51	·7076	7084	7093	7101	7110	7118	7126	7135	7143	7152	1	2	3	3	4	5	6	7	8
52	·7160	7168	7177	7185	7193	7202	7210	7218	7226	7235	1	2	2	3	4	5	6	7	7
53	·7243	7251	7259	7267	7275	7284	7292	7300	7308	7316	1	2	2	3	4	5	6	6	7
54	·7324	7332	7340	7348	7356	7364	7372	7380	7388	7396	1	2	2	3	4	5	6	6	7

LOGARITHMS

	0	1	2	3	4	5	6	7	8	9	1	2	3	4	5	6	7	8	9
55	·7404	7412	7419	7427	7435	7443	7451	7459	7466	7474	1	2	2	3	4	5	5	6	7
56	·7482	7490	7497	7505	7513	7520	7528	7536	7543	7551	1	2	2	3	4	5	5	6	7
57	·7559	7566	7574	7582	7589	7597	7604	7612	7619	7627	1	2	2	3	4	5	5	6	7
58	·7634	7642	7649	7657	7664	7672	7679	7686	7694	7701	1	1	2	3	4	4	5	6	7
59	·7709	7716	7723	7731	7738	7745	7752	7760	7767	7774	1	1	2	3	4	4	5	6	7
60	·7782	7789	7796	7803	7810	7818	7825	7832	7839	7846	1	1	2	3	4	4	5	6	6
61	·7853	7860	7868	7875	7882	7889	7896	7903	7910	7917	1	1	2	3	4	4	5	6	6
62	·7924	7931	7938	7945	7952	7959	7966	7973	7980	7987	1	1	2	3	3	4	5	6	6
63	·7993	8000	8007	8014	8021	8028	8035	8041	8048	8055	1	1	2	3	3	4	5	5	6
64	·8062	8069	8075	8082	8089	8096	8102	8109	8116	8122	1	1	2	3	3	4	5	5	6
65	·8129	8136	8142	8149	8156	8162	8169	8176	8182	8189	1	1	2	3	3	4	5	5	6
66	·8195	8202	8209	8215	8222	8228	8235	8241	8248	8254	1	1	2	3	3	4	5	5	6
67	·8261	8267	8274	8280	8287	8293	8299	8306	8312	8319	1	1	2	3	3	4	5	5	6
68	·8325	8331	8338	8344	8351	8357	8363	8370	8376	8382	1	1	2	3	3	4	4	5	6
69	·8388	8395	8401	8407	8414	8420	8426	8432	8439	8445	1	1	2	2	3	4	4	5	6
70	·8451	8457	8463	8470	8476	8482	8488	8494	8500	8506	1	1	2	2	3	4	4	5	6
71	·8513	8519	8525	8531	8537	8543	8549	8555	8561	8567	1	1	2	2	3	4	4	5	5
72	·8573	8579	8585	8591	8597	8603	8609	8615	8621	8627	1	1	2	2	3	4	4	5	5
73	·8633	8639	8645	8651	8657	8663	8669	8675	8681	8686	1	1	2	2	3	4	4	5	5
74	·8692	8698	8704	8710	8716	8722	8727	8733	8739	8745	1	1	2	2	3	4	4	5	5
75	·8751	8756	8762	8768	8774	8779	8785	8791	8797	8802	1	1	2	2	3	3	4	5	5
76	·8808	8814	8820	8825	8831	8837	8842	8848	8854	8859	1	1	2	2	3	3	4	5	5
77	·8865	8871	8876	8882	8887	8893	8899	8904	8910	8915	1	1	2	2	3	3	4	4	5
78	·8921	8927	8932	8938	8943	8949	8954	8960	8965	8971	1	1	2	2	3	3	4	4	5
79	·8976	8982	8987	8993	8998	9004	9009	9015	9020	9025	1	1	2	2	3	3	4	4	5
80	·9031	9036	9042	9047	9053	9058	9063	9069	9074	9079	1	1	2	2	3	3	4	4	5
81	·9085	9090	9096	9101	9106	9112	9117	9122	9128	9133	1	1	2	2	3	3	4	4	5
82	·9138	9143	9149	9154	9159	9165	9170	9175	9180	9186	1	1	2	2	3	3	4	4	5
83	·9191	9196	9201	9206	9212	9217	9222	9227	9232	9238	1	1	2	2	3	3	4	4	5
84	·9243	9248	9253	9258	9263	9269	9274	9279	9284	9289	1	1	2	2	3	3	4	4	5
85	·9294	9299	9304	9309	9315	9320	9325	9330	9335	9340	1	1	2	2	3	3	4	4	5
86	·9345	9350	9355	9360	9365	9370	9375	9380	9385	9390	1	1	2	2	3	3	4	4	5
87	·9395	9400	9405	9410	9415	9420	9425	9430	9435	9440	0	1	1	2	2	3	3	4	4
88	·9445	9450	9455	9460	9465	9469	9474	9479	9484	9489	0	1	1	2	2	3	3	4	4
89	·9494	9499	9504	9509	9513	9518	9523	9528	9533	9538	0	1	1	2	2	3	3	4	4
90	·9542	9547	9552	9557	9562	9566	9571	9576	9581	9586	0	1	1	2	2	3	3	4	4
91	·9590	9595	9600	9605	9609	9614	9619	9624	9628	9633	0	1	1	2	2	3	3	4	4
92	·9638	9643	9647	9652	9657	9661	9666	9671	9675	9680	0	1	1	2	2	3	3	4	4
93	·9685	9689	9694	9699	9703	9708	9713	9717	9722	9727	0	1	1	2	2	3	3	4	4
94	·9731	9736	9741	9745	9750	9754	9759	9763	9768	9773	0	1	1	2	2	3	3	4	4
95	·9777	9782	9786	9791	9795	9800	9805	9809	9814	9818	0	1	1	2	2	3	3	4	4
96	·9823	9827	9832	9836	9841	9845	9850	9854	9859	9863	0	1	1	2	2	3	3	4	4
97	·9868	9872	9877	9881	9886	9890	9894	9899	9903	9908	0	1	1	2	2	3	3	4	4
98	·9912	9917	9921	9926	9930	9934	9939	9943	9948	9952	0	1	1	2	2	3	3	4	4
99	·9956	9961	9965	9969	9974	9978	9983	9987	9991	9996	0	1	1	2	2	3	3	3	4

ANTI-LOGARITHMS

	0	1	2	3	4	5	6	7	8	9	1	2	3	4	5	6	7	8	9
·00	1000	1002	1005	1007	1009	1012	1014	1016	1019	1021	0	0	1	1	1	1	2	2	2
·01	1023	1026	1028	1030	1033	1035	1038	1040	1042	1045	0	0	1	1	1	1	2	2	2
·02	1047	1050	1052	1054	1057	1059	1062	1064	1067	1069	0	0	1	1	1	1	2	2	2
·03	1072	1074	1076	1079	1081	1084	1086	1089	1091	1094	0	0	1	1	1	1	2	2	2
·04	1096	1099	1102	1104	1107	1109	1112	1114	1117	1119	0	1	1	1	1	2	2	2	2
·05	1122	1125	1127	1130	1132	1135	1138	1140	1143	1146	0	1	1	1	1	2	2	2	2
·06	1148	1151	1153	1156	1159	1161	1164	1167	1169	1172	0	1	1	1	1	2	2	2	2
·07	1175	1178	1180	1183	1186	1189	1191	1194	1197	1199	0	1	1	1	1	2	2	2	2
·08	1202	1205	1208	1211	1213	1216	1219	1222	1225	1227	0	1	1	1	1	2	2	2	3
·09	1230	1233	1236	1239	1242	1245	1247	1250	1253	1256	0	1	1	1	1	2	2	2	3
·10	1259	1262	1265	1268	1271	1274	1276	1279	1282	1285	0	1	1	1	1	2	2	2	3
·11	1288	1291	1294	1297	1300	1303	1306	1309	1312	1315	0	1	1	1	2	2	2	2	3
·12	1318	1321	1324	1327	1330	1334	1337	1340	1343	1346	0	1	1	1	2	2	2	3	3
·13	1349	1352	1355	1358	1361	1365	1368	1371	1374	1377	0	1	1	1	2	2	2	3	3
·14	1380	1384	1387	1390	1393	1396	1400	1403	1406	1409	0	1	1	1	2	2	2	3	3
·15	1413	1416	1419	1422	1426	1429	1432	1435	1439	1442	0	1	1	1	2	2	2	3	3
·16	1445	1449	1452	1455	1459	1462	1466	1469	1472	1476	0	1	1	1	2	2	2	3	3
·17	1479	1483	1486	1489	1493	1496	1500	1503	1507	1510	0	1	1	1	2	2	2	3	3
·18	1514	1517	1521	1524	1528	1531	1535	1538	1542	1545	0	1	1	1	2	2	2	3	3
·19	1549	1552	1556	1560	1563	1567	1570	1574	1578	1581	0	1	1	1	2	2	3	3	3
·20	1585	1589	1592	1596	1600	1603	1607	1611	1614	1618	0	1	1	2	2	2	3	3	3
·21	1622	1626	1629	1633	1637	1641	1644	1648	1652	1656	0	1	1	2	2	2	3	3	3
·22	1660	1663	1667	1671	1675	1679	1683	1687	1690	1694	0	1	1	2	2	2	3	3	3
·23	1698	1702	1706	1710	1714	1718	1722	1726	1730	1734	0	1	1	2	2	2	3	3	4
·24	1738	1742	1746	1750	1754	1758	1762	1766	1770	1774	0	1	1	2	2	2	3	3	4
·25	1778	1782	1786	1791	1795	1799	1803	1807	1811	1816	0	1	1	2	2	2	3	3	4
·26	1820	1824	1828	1832	1837	1841	1845	1849	1854	1858	0	1	1	2	2	3	3	3	4
·27	1862	1866	1871	1875	1879	1884	1888	1892	1897	1901	0	1	1	2	2	3	3	3	4
·28	1905	1910	1914	1919	1923	1928	1932	1936	1941	1945	0	1	1	2	2	3	3	4	4
·29	1950	1954	1959	1963	1968	1972	1977	1982	1986	1991	0	1	1	2	2	3	3	4	4
·30	1995	2000	2004	2009	2014	2018	2023	2028	2032	2037	0	1	1	2	2	3	3	4	4
·31	2042	2046	2051	2056	2061	2065	2070	2075	2080	2084	0	1	1	2	2	3	3	4	4
·32	2089	2094	2099	2104	2109	2113	2118	2123	2128	2133	0	1	1	2	2	3	3	4	4
·33	2138	2143	2148	2153	2158	2163	2168	2173	2178	2183	0	1	1	2	2	3	3	4	4
·34	2188	2193	2198	2203	2208	2213	2218	2223	2228	2234	1	1	2	2	3	3	4	4	5
·35	2239	2244	2249	2254	2259	2265	2270	2275	2280	2286	1	1	2	2	3	3	4	4	5
·36	2291	2296	2301	2307	2312	2317	2323	2328	2333	2339	1	1	2	2	3	3	4	4	5
·37	2344	2350	2355	2360	2366	2371	2377	2382	2388	2393	1	1	2	2	3	3	4	4	5
·38	2399	2404	2410	2415	2421	2427	2432	2438	2443	2449	1	1	2	2	3	3	4	4	5
·39	2455	2460	2466	2472	2477	2483	2489	2495	2500	2506	1	1	2	2	3	3	4	5	5
·40	2512	2518	2523	2529	2535	2541	2547	2553	2559	2564	1	1	2	2	3	4	4	5	5
·41	2570	2576	2582	2588	2594	2600	2606	2612	2618	2624	1	1	2	2	3	4	4	5	5
·42	2630	2636	2642	2649	2655	2661	2667	2673	2679	2685	1	1	2	2	3	4	4	5	6
·43	2692	2698	2704	2710	2716	2723	2729	2735	2742	2748	1	1	2	2	3	4	4	5	6
·44	2754	2761	2767	2773	2780	2786	2793	2799	2805	2812	1	1	2	3	3	4	4	5	6
·45	2818	2825	2831	2838	2844	2851	2858	2864	2871	2877	1	1	2	3	3	4	5	5	6
·46	2884	2891	2897	2904	2911	2917	2924	2931	2938	2944	1	1	2	3	3	4	5	5	6
·47	2951	2958	2965	2972	2979	2985	2992	2999	3006	3013	1	1	2	3	3	4	5	5	6
·48	3020	3027	3034	3041	3048	3055	3062	3069	3076	3083	1	1	2	3	4	4	5	6	6
·49	3090	3097	3105	3112	3119	3126	3133	3141	3148	3155	1	1	2	3	4	4	5	6	6

ANTI-LOGARITHMS

	0	1	2	3	4	5	6	7	8	9	1	2	3	4	5	6	7	8	9
·50	3162	3170	3177	3184	3192	3199	3206	3214	3221	3228	1	1	2	3	4	4	5	6	7
·51	3236	3243	3251	3258	3266	3273	3281	3289	3296	3304	1	2	2	3	4	5	5	6	7
·52	3311	3319	3327	3334	3342	3350	3357	3365	3373	3381	1	2	2	3	4	5	5	6	7
·53	3388	3396	3404	3412	3420	3428	3436	3443	3451	3459	1	2	2	3	4	5	6	6	7
·54	3467	3475	3483	3491	3499	3508	3516	3524	3532	3540	1	2	2	3	4	5	6	6	7
·55	3548	3556	3565	3573	3581	3589	3597	3606	3614	3622	1	2	2	3	4	5	6	7	7
·56	3631	3639	3648	3656	3664	3673	3681	3690	3698	3707	1	2	3	3	4	5	6	7	8
·57	3715	3724	3733	3741	3750	3758	3767	3776	3784	3793	1	2	3	3	4	5	6	7	8
·58	3802	3811	3819	3828	3837	3846	3855	3864	3873	3882	1	2	3	4	4	5	6	7	8
·59	3890	3899	3908	3917	3926	3936	3945	3954	3963	3972	1	2	3	4	5	5	6	7	8
·60	3981	3990	3999	4009	4018	4027	4036	4046	4055	4064	1	2	3	4	5	6	6	7	8
·61	4074	4083	4093	4102	4111	4121	4130	4140	4150	4159	1	2	3	4	5	6	7	8	9
·62	4169	4178	4188	4198	4207	4217	4227	4236	4246	4256	1	2	3	4	5	6	7	8	9
·63	4266	4276	4285	4295	4305	4315	4325	4335	4345	4355	1	2	3	4	5	6	7	8	9
·64	4365	4375	4385	4395	4406	4416	4426	4436	4446	4457	1	2	3	4	5	6	7	8	9
·65	4467	4477	4487	4498	4508	4519	4529	4539	4550	4560	1	2	3	4	5	6	7	8	9
·66	4571	4581	4592	4603	4613	4624	4634	4645	4656	4667	1	2	3	4	5	6	7	9	10
·67	4677	4688	4699	4710	4721	4732	4742	4753	4764	4775	1	2	3	4	5	7	8	9	10
·68	4786	4797	4808	4819	4831	4842	4853	4864	4875	4887	1	2	3	4	6	7	8	9	10
·69	4898	4909	4920	4932	4943	4955	4966	4977	4989	5000	1	2	3	5	6	7	8	9	10
·70	5012	5023	5035	5047	5058	5070	5082	5093	5105	5117	1	2	4	5	6	7	8	9	11
·71	5129	5140	5152	5164	5176	5188	5200	5212	5224	5236	1	2	4	5	6	7	8	10	11
·72	5248	5260	5272	5284	5297	5309	5321	5333	5346	5358	1	2	4	5	6	7	9	10	11
·73	5370	5383	5395	5408	5420	5433	5445	5458	5470	5483	1	3	4	5	6	8	9	10	11
·74	5495	5508	5521	5534	5546	5559	5572	5585	5598	5610	1	3	4	5	6	8	9	10	12
·75	5623	5636	5649	5662	5675	5689	5702	5715	5728	5741	1	3	4	5	7	8	9	10	12
·76	5754	5768	5781	5794	5808	5821	5834	5848	5861	5875	1	3	4	5	7	8	9	11	12
·77	5888	5902	5916	5929	5943	5957	5970	5984	5998	6012	1	3	4	5	7	8	10	11	12
·78	6026	6039	6053	6067	6081	6095	6109	6124	6138	6152	1	3	4	6	7	8	10	11	13
·79	6166	6180	6194	6209	6223	6237	6252	6266	6281	6295	1	3	4	6	7	9	10	11	13
·80	6310	6324	6339	6353	6368	6383	6397	6412	6427	6442	1	3	4	6	7	9	10	12	13
·81	6457	6471	6486	6501	6516	6531	6546	6561	6577	6592	2	3	5	6	8	9	11	12	14
·82	6607	6622	6637	6653	6668	6683	6699	6714	6730	6745	2	3	5	6	8	9	11	12	14
·83	6761	6776	6792	6808	6823	6839	6855	6871	6887	6902	2	3	5	6	8	9	11	13	14
·84	6918	6934	6950	6966	6982	6998	7015	7031	7047	7063	2	3	5	6	8	10	11	13	15
·85	7079	7096	7112	7129	7145	7161	7178	7194	7211	7228	2	3	5	7	8	10	12	13	15
·86	7244	7261	7278	7295	7311	7328	7345	7362	7379	7396	2	3	5	7	8	10	12	13	15
·87	7413	7430	7447	7464	7482	7499	7516	7534	7551	7568	2	3	5	7	9	10	12	14	16
·88	7586	7603	7621	7638	7656	7674	7691	7709	7727	7745	2	4	5	7	9	11	12	14	16
·89	7762	7780	7798	7816	7834	7852	7870	7889	7907	7925	2	4	5	7	9	11	13	14	16
·90	7943	7962	7980	7998	8017	8035	8054	8072	8091	8110	2	4	6	7	9	11	13	15	17
·91	8128	8147	8166	8185	8204	8222	8241	8260	8279	8299	2	4	6	8	9	11	13	15	17
·92	8318	8337	8356	8375	8395	8414	8433	8453	8472	8492	2	4	6	8	10	12	14	15	17
·93	8511	8531	8551	8570	8590	8610	8630	8650	8670	8690	2	4	6	8	10	12	14	16	18
·94	8710	8730	8750	8770	8790	8810	8831	8851	8872	8892	2	4	6	8	10	12	14	16	18
·95	8913	8933	8954	8974	8995	9016	9036	9057	9078	9099	2	4	6	8	10	12	15	17	19
·96	9120	9141	9162	9183	9204	9226	9247	9268	9290	9311	2	4	6	8	11	13	15	17	19
·97	9333	9354	9376	9397	9419	9441	9462	9484	9506	9528	2	4	7	9	11	13	15	17	20
·98	9550	9572	9594	9616	9638	9661	9683	9705	9727	9750	2	4	7	9	11	13	16	18	20
·99	9772	9795	9817	9840	9863	9886	9908	9931	9954	9977	2	5	7	9	11	14	16	18	20

Atomic Weight (Relative Atomic Mass) Tables

ATOMIC WEIGHTS (RELATIVE ATOMIC MASSES)

ELEMENT	SYMBOL	ATOMIC WEIGHT (RAM)		ATOMIC NUMBER	MELTING POINT Celsius (Kelvin = Celsius + 273)	DENSITY (kg/m³) (× 10³)	VALENCY (oxidation state)
		Exact	For calculations				
Actinium	Ac	227	—	89	—	—	3
Aluminium	Al	26·98	27	13	660	2·7	3
Americium	Am	243	—	95	850	11·7	3
Antimony	Sb	121·76	—	51	630	6·7	3, 5
Argon	A or Ar	39·942	—	18	−189	(1·4)	—
Arsenic	As	74·91	—	33	(814)	5·7	3, 5
Astatine	At	211	—	85	—	—	1
Barium	Ba	137·36	137	56	725	3·5	2
Berkelium	Bk	249	—	97	—	—	3
Beryllium	Be	9·013	—	4	1280	1·8	2
Bismuth	Bi	209·00	—	83	271	9·8	3, 5
Boron	B	10·82	—	5	2300	3·3	3
Bromine	Br	79·913	80	35	−7	3·1	1
Cadmium	Cd	112·41	—	48	321	8·6	2
Caesium	Cs	132·91	—	55	28	1·9	1
Calcium	Ca	40·08	40	20	842	1·5	2
Californium	Cf	249	—	98	—	—	3
Carbon	C	12·011	12	6	3500	3·5	4
Cerium	Ce	140·13	—	58	800	6·7	3, 4
Chlorine	Cl	35·455	35·5	17	−101	(1·9)	1
Chromium	Cr	52·01	52	24	1890	7·2	3, 6
Cobalt	Co	58·94	—	27	1495	8·9	2
Copper	Cu	63·54	63·5	29	1083	8·9	1, 2
Curium	Cm	245	—	96	—	—	3
Dysprosium	Dy	162·51	—	66	—	—	3
Einsteinium	Es	254	—	99	—	—	3
Erbium	Er	167·27	—	68	—	—	3
Europium	Eu	152·0	—	63	1150	—	3
Fermium	Fm	255	—	100	—	—	3
Fluorine	F	19·00	—	9	−223	(1·1)	1
Francium	Fr	223	—	87	—	—	1

(new standard, $^{12}C = 12·0000$)

ATOMIC WEIGHTS (RELATIVE ATOMIC MASSES)

ELEMENT	SYMBOL	ATOMIC WEIGHT (RAM)		ATOMIC NUMBER	MELTING POINT Celsius (Kelvin = Celsius + 273)	DENSITY (kg/m³) (× 10³)	VALENCY (oxidation state)
		Exact	For calculations				
Gadolinium	Gd	157·26	—	64	—	—	3
Gallium	Ga	69·72	—	31	30	5·9	3
Germanium	Ge	72·60	—	32	·960	5·3	4
Gold	Au	197·0	—·	79	1063	19·3	1, 3
Hafnium	Hf	178·50	—	72	1700	13·3	4
Helium	He	4·003	—	2	−272	(0·2)	—
Holmium	Ho	164·94	—	67	—	—	3
Hydrogen	H	1·0080	1	1	−259	(0·1)	1
Indium	In	114·82	—	49	156	7·3	3
Iodine	I	126·91	127	53	114	4·9	1
Iridium	Ir	192·2	—	77	2450	22·4	3
Iron	Fe	55·85	56	26	1535	7·9	2, 3
Krypton	Kr	83·80	—	36	−157	(2·2)	—
Lanthanum	La	138·92	—	57	826	6·2	3
Lawrencium	Lw	—	—	103	—	—	3
Lead	Pb	207·20	207	82	327	11·3	2, 4
Lithium	Li	6·940	—	3	186	0·5	1
Lutecium	Lu	174·99	—	71	—	9·7	3
Magnesium	Mg	24·32	24	12	651	1·7	2
Manganese	Mn	54·94	55	25	1260	7·2	2, 7
Mendelevium	Mv	256	—	101	—	—	3
Mercury	Hg	200·60	—	80	−39	13·5	1, 2
Molybdenum	Mo	95·95	—	42	2620	10·2	3, 6
Neodymium	Nd	144·27	—	60	840	6·9	3
Neon	Ne	20·182	—	10	−249	(1·2)	—
Neptunium	Np	237	—	93	640	20·5	4, 5
Nickel	Ni	58·71	—	28	1455	8·9	2
Niobium	Nb	92·91	—	41	2500	8·6	3, 5
Nitrogen	N	14·008	14	7	−210	(0·8)	3
Nobelium	No	256	—	102	—	—	3
Osmium	Os	190·2	—	76	2700	22·5	4, 8
Oxygen	O	15·9993	16	8	−218	(1·1)	2
Palladium	Pd	106·4	—	46	1550	12·0	2, 4
Phosphorus	P	30·974	31	15	44	1·8	3, 5
Platinum	Pt	195·08	—	78	1773	21·5	2, 4
Plutonium	Pu	242	—	94	635	16·0	4

ATOMIC WEIGHTS (RELATIVE ATOMIC MASSES)

ELEMENT	SYMBOL	ATOMIC WEIGHT (RAM)		ATOMIC NUMBER	MELTING POINT Celsius (Kelvin = Celsius + 273)	DENSITY (kg/m³) (× 10³)	VALENCY (oxidation state)
		Exact	For calculations				
Polonium	Po	210	—	84	—	—	2
Potassium	K	39·100	39	19	62	0·9	1
Praseodymium	Pr	140·92	—	59	940	6·5	3
Prometheum	Pm	145	—	61	—	—	3
Protoactinium	Pa	231	—	91	—	—	5
Radium	Ra	226·04	—	88	700	5·0	2
Radon	Rn	222	—	86	−71	(4·4)	—
Rhenium	Re	186·22	—	75	3200	20·5	4, 7
Rhodium	Rh	102·91	—	45	1970	12·4	3
Rubidium	Rb	85·48	—	37	38	1·5	1
Ruthenium	Ru	101·1	—	44	1950	12·6	3, 8
Samarium	Sm	150·35	—	62	1300	7·7	3
Scandium	Sc	44·96	—	21	1200	2·5	3
Selenium	Se	78·96	—	34	220	4·8	2, 6
Silicon	Si	28·09	28	14	1420	2·4	4
Silver	Ag	107·876	108	47	960	10·5	1
Sodium	Na	22·991	23	11	97	0·9	1
Strontium	Sr	87·63	—	38	774	2·6	2
Sulphur	S	32·065	32	16	119	2·1	2, 6
Tantalum	Ta	180·95	—	73	3000	16·6	5
Technetium	Tc	99	—	43	—	—	4, 7
Tellurium	Te	127·61	—	52	450	6·2	2, 6
Terbium	Tb	158·93	—	65	330	—	3
Thallium	Tl	204·38	—	81	302	11·9	1, 3
Thorium	Th	232·04	—	90	1845	11·2	4
Thulium	Tm	168·94	—	69	—	—	3
Tin	Sn	118·70	—	50	232	7·3	2, 4
Titanium	Ti	47·90	—	22	1800	4·5	3, 4
Tungsten	W	183·86	—	74	3370	19·3	6
Uranium	U	238·07	—	92	1133	18·7	4, 6
Vanadium	V	50·95	—	23	1710	6·0	3, 5
Xenon	Xe	131·3	—	54	−112	(3·5)	—
Ytterbium	Yb	173·04	—	70	1800	—	3
Yttrium	Y	88·92	—	39	1490	5·5	3
Zinc	Zn	65·38	65	30	419	7·1	2
Zirconium	Zr	91·22	—	40	1860	6·4	4